FILING
SYSTEMS
AND
RECORDS
MANAGEMENT

College Series
Third Edition

Gregg Division
McGraw-Hill Book Company
New York   Atlanta   Dallas
St. Louis   San Francisco   Auckland
Bogotá   Guatemala   Hamburg
Johannesburg   Lisbon   London
Madrid   Mexico   Montreal
New Delhi   Panama   Paris
San Juan   São Paulo   Singapore
Sydney   Tokyo   Toronto

FILING SYSTEMS AND RECORDS MANAGEMENT

Jeffrey R. Stewart, Jr., Ed.D.
Professor of Business Education
Virginia Polytechnic Institute and State University
Blacksburg, Virginia

Judith A. Scharle, M.S.
Adult Education Specialist
Norfolk Public Schools
Norfolk, Virginia

Judith A. Hickey, M. A.
Associate Professor, Division of Business
Thomas Nelson Community College
Hampton, Virginia

Gilbert Kahn, Ed.D.
Late Professor of Business Education
Montclair State College
Upper Montclair, New Jersey

Sponsoring Editor	Ella Pezzuti
Editing Supervisor	Gloria Schlein
Production Supervisor	Priscilla Taguer
Design Supervisor	Nancy Axelrod
Art Supervisor	George T. Resch
Cover Illustrator	Tom Christopher
Technical Studio	Fine Line Inc.

Library of Congress Cataloging in Publication Data
Main entry under title:

Filing systems and records management.

  (College series)
  Second ed. (1971) by G. Kahn, T. Yerian, and
J. R. Stewart, Jr.
  Includes index.
  1. Files and filing (Documents) 2. Business
records. I. Stewart, Jeffrey Robert, date.
II. Kahn, Gilbert, date. Filing systems and
records management.
HF5736.K283   1981   651.5   80-21605
ISBN 0–07–061471–7

Filing Systems and Records Management, Third Edition, College Series

90 DODO 89876

ISBN 0-07-061471-7

PREFACE

Whether a student will be employed in a secretarial, stenographic, typing, accounting, word processing, data processing, micrographics, or records management job, *Filing Systems and Records Management, Third Edition,* presents information and the opportunity to obtain skills needed to handle paperwork in any of these office occupations. Its companion, *Practice Materials for Filing Systems and Records Management, Third Edition,* provides realistic jobs for the development of knowledge and skill in filing and managing records.

Specific competencies are listed at the beginning of each chapter of the text, with additional competencies indicated for accomplishment by those students who use the *Practice Materials.* Thus practice for each competency is provided in the text, the *Practice Materials,* or both. It is easy for the student and the instructor to select those competencies that are most applicable to the office position being sought by the student. It is therefore convenient to tailor the filing course to individual students' needs, making the program adaptable to a variety of teaching situations—community college, adult education, four-year institution, and in-service training programs for office workers.

FEATURES

Business educators are continually faced with numerous advancements in office technology. In addition, instructors must deal with new teaching delivery systems for a wide range of student interests and backgrounds. For these reasons, the authors have included several new elements in this edition that reflect changes in both technology and instructional approaches.

COMPETENCY-BASED PROGRAM.   *Filing Systems and Records Management, Third Edition,* and *Practice Materials for Filing Systems and Records Management, Third Edition,* provide a thorough, competency-based course that includes:

1. Statements of filing and records management competencies needed by office workers.
2. Text material and realistic practice materials designed to enable students to meet those competencies.

3. A complete testing program, including both performance and objective tests, to reinforce and evaluate the achievement of those competencies.

PRESENTATION OF INDEXING RULES. The newly revised indexing rules appear in two chapters. Chapter 2 deals with the indexing rules for names of individuals; Chapter 3 presents those indexing rules which apply to business, organization, and special names. The rules are presented so that students will have the opportunity to practice a few rules at a time. The indexing rules are considered progressively—from the least complex rule to those which are more complex.

ORGANIZATION OF THE WORK STATION. New to this edition, the organization of the office worker's individual work station is discussed in Chapter 11. The authors have determined that basic organization is essential to overall worker efficiency and represents a significant filing and records management activity for most office workers. This chapter deals with reference books, follow-up, log books, and priority setting, as well as with both the desk top and the desk-drawer file.

RELATED PRACTICE MATERIALS. *Practice Materials for Filing Systems and Records Management, Third Edition,* has been developed and correlated with *Filing Systems and Records Management, Third Edition.* It contains practice materials for use by the student to obtain skills in the following functions of filing and records management: (1) alphabetic card filing, (2) alphabetic correspondence filing, (3) numeric card filing, (4) numeric correspondence filing, (5) subject card filing, (6) subject correspondence filing, (7) geographic card filing, (8) geographic correspondence filing, (9) transferring, and (10) follow-up activities. Retrieval, charging out, and basic procedures for all systems are included. The *Practice Materials* include the cards, miniature letters, answer sheets, and all other supplies necessary to complete the jobs. Performance tests are also included in the *Practice Materials.*

SUPPORTING MATERIALS

The publications listed here are available and may be used as supplementary materials with *Filing Systems and Records Management, Third Edition,* and with the *Practice Materials for Filing Systems and Records Management, Third Edition.*

1. *Gregg Filing Transparencies, Volume I: Alphabetic Indexing,* presents the twenty-five indexing rules as well as illustrated instructions for steps in card filing, typing captions on file cards, and cross-referencing in card files.
2. *Gregg Filing Transparencies, Volume II: Systems and Procedures,* contains illustrations and teacher's guide notes on filing systems and procedures, including alphabetic, numeric, subject, and geographic.

3. *Workbook Exercises in Alphabetic Filing, Third Edition,* provides file cards containing over 650 names for extensive practice in the application of the twenty-five indexing rules.
4. *Instructor's Manual and Key for Filing Systems and Records Management, Third Edition,* includes teaching suggestions, alternate time schedules, and a complete key to the text, the *Practice Materials,* and the objective tests. The objective tests are provided with permission for instructors to reproduce them for their classes.

The primary goal of *Filing Systems and Records Management, Third Edition,* is to prepare the student to become a skilled and knowledgeable filing and records management employee able to succeed in an important area of office operations. This competency-based program contains complete materials to meet that goal.

Jeffrey R. Stewart, Jr.
Judith A. Scharle
Judith A. Hickey

CONTENTS

1

Challenges, Concepts, Careers

COMPETENCIES

When you have completed this chapter, you will be able to:

1. State why filing and records management is important to you.
2. Define the terms *filing* and *records management.*
3. State why records are necessary and give examples of records needed by businesses and individuals.
4. Name the two basic methods used for filing.
5. Define the terms *records, correspondence, filing system, system, procedure, method,* and *caption.*
6. List the four classifications businesses use to value their records and give examples of each classification.
7. List and describe the stages in the life cycle of a business record.
8. Compare the Freedom of Information Act with the Privacy Act, and state why each is important in filing.
9. State why the *need to know* is important to the file worker.
10. State why office employees need to have a knowledge of filing.
11. Name five job titles in filing and records management and list two duties of each.

WHY LEARN ABOUT FILING AND RECORDS MANAGEMENT

At one time, records management was considered to mean the storage, retrieval, and protection of business papers—basically *filing*. Today, *records management* includes not only filing but the creation, control, use, and disposition of records.

Records management and filing are not the responsibilities of just one person or department in a business. They are the responsibilities of everyone who handles business records. All office workers need to be aware of the importance of correct creation, storage, protection, control, use, and disposition of records.

For this reason, it is important that you study carefully the information presented in this textbook. It will help you handle your filing and records management responsibilities on the job. Failure to classify, store, and retrieve records accurately and efficiently can result in records lost forever, which can be a serious loss to an organization.

WHY RECORDS ARE NECESSARY

Records are necessary because they contain all the information vital to the day-to-day operation of the business or organization. Without records, a business cannot function. Studies have shown that many businesses that lose their records through fire, disaster, or negligence cease to operate. When government agencies lose records, it often creates a hardship on private individuals who may need these records to prove date of birth, date of military discharge, or ownership of property. Medical records may be necessary years later for reference or for identification purposes. You may have wanted to return a defective piece of merchandise, but you found you did not have the original sales slip to prove the price paid and the date of purchase. You may have wanted to refer to an item you had saved, but you could not find it. For you, this may have been merely an annoyance; when a business cannot find records, it costs money and goodwill. Businesses and individuals need to keep complete, accurate records for tax purposes. Failure to comply with the tax laws may result in fines or, in extreme cases, in prison sentences. Accurate records of earnings, expenses, and deductions can result in substantial savings by avoiding the overpayment of taxes.

BASIC METHODS OF FILING

Before you started this formal study of filing, you had already become familiar with some of the basic methods of filing. Each time you looked for a number in the telephone directory, you used alphabetic filing because names are arranged alphabetically and your knowledge of the alphabet helped you find the name you wanted. Thus the telephone directory is an example of one of the two basic methods of arranging records—by name. The other basic method is by number. If you or someone in your family has a checking account, you may have arranged canceled checks by number so that you could reconcile your bank statement each month. The bank would probably arrange canceled checks in order by the account number. Insurance companies and lawyers' offices are examples of businesses that frequently use numbers for filing their records. Educational institutions, hospitals, government agencies, and most businesses file records alphabetically by names.

TERMS.   The information business needs to carry on vital activities is contained in various business *records* which are stored in *filing systems*. *Records* refers to all the information that is kept by an organization. It may be in the form of correspondence, cards, tapes, or microfilms. *Correspondence* is the term which refers to any written communication that has not been designed to be placed in a card or forms file.

A *system* is a series of related steps followed in accomplishing a major office activity. A *filing system* is an arrangement of equipment and supplies to permit the storing of records according to a definite plan. A *procedure* is a series of related substeps performed to carry out part of the system. A *method* is the breakdown of a procedure into the steps by which it is accomplished.

A *caption* is a name or number used to identify records for filing purposes. For example, if a letter is to be kept in the Rogers Hardware Store file, the name of the store would be the caption. A caption is typed on a folder label.

CAPTIONS FOR DIFFERENT FILING SYSTEMS.   An alphabetic filing system would use business and special organization names (such as names of hotels, hospitals, educational institutions) and/or individual names as captions. Examples of alphabetic captions are *Kendall; Kendall, Andrew R.;* and *Kendall Motor Company*. A subject filing system would use the names of items or objects as captions. Examples of subject captions are *Typewriters;* and *Repairs: Typewriters*. A numeric system assigns numbers to the business or special names and individual names. For example, Andrew R. Kendall might be assigned File No. 350; Kendall Motor Company, File No. 385. Since these captions do not readily reveal the contents of the folder, an alphabetic card index is usually part of the numeric filing system. A geographic system would use as captions the names of places or locations such as cities, towns, counties, states, or countries. Examples of geographic filing captions are *Rochester, New York: Adams Company; Seattle, Washington: Archer Imports*.

HOW BUSINESSES CLASSIFY THE VALUE OF RECORDS

In determining the value of their records and how long they should be kept, many businesses analyze and classify them as follows:

VITAL RECORDS.   These include legal papers of incorporation, titles to ownership, deeds, major contracts, property plans, reports to stockholders, minutes of directors' meetings, and insurance policies. They should never be destroyed because they are essential to the existence of the organization and are often irreplaceable.

IMPORTANT RECORDS.   These include invoices, accounts receivable, sales records, quotations, financial statements, tax records, and certain correspondence. They facilitate the routine of the business and are replaceable only at great cost and with much delay. If they are not being used, they may be transferred to inactive storage space and placed in containers that will keep them in good condition.

USEFUL RECORDS.   These include some general correspondence, memorandums, and bank statements. They are temporarily helpful and are replaceable at slight cost. They are often destroyed from a few weeks to a year after they are received.

NONESSENTIAL PAPERS.   These include routine inquiries, announcements, and acknowledgments. They should never be filed with more important records, and they may be destroyed after temporary use.

LIFE CYCLE OF A BUSINESS RECORD

A knowledgeable businessperson is not only concerned with how records make it possible to run a business at a profit; that person is also aware of the complete life cycle of each record and knows that some provision must be made for the eventual transfer and disposition of records. (See the illustration below.)

The life cycle of a business record has five stages: (1) creation or receipt, (2) storage and protection, (3) use, (4) transfer, and (5) disposal.

LIFE CYCLE OF A BUSINESS RECORD

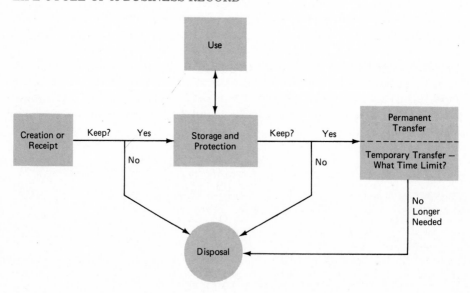

CREATION OR RECEIPT. The number of records handled daily within a typical organization is staggering. A large retail store, for example, will create hundreds of records every day—letters, advertising copy, accounting statements, purchase orders, sales slips, checks, receiving tickets, and so on. Also, the same store receives hundreds, perhaps thousands, of pieces of correspondence daily—applications for credit, invoices, order letters, credit reports, price lists, catalogs, and so on. Hundreds of worker-hours are spent daily in handling these records. Without the records the business simply could not operate. Most records eventually find their way into one type of file or another so that they may be referred to when needed as a basis for important managerial decisions and action.

STORAGE AND PROTECTION. When the decision is made to retain business papers, provision must be made for storing and protecting them during their useful lifetime. Because of their unusual size or shape, records such as large blueprints in an architect's office require equipment especially made for storing them. Extremely important records, such as legal papers, are stored in insulated cabinets capable of withstanding extreme heat in case of fire. Any record worth retaining should be properly housed so that it can be located rapidly when needed and so that it is always adequately protected.

USE. Records are stored for one principal reason: use. Only records that will be needed for later reference are worth the time required to store them. Office space and filing equipment are too expensive to be used to "hide" papers that no one will ever use. Knowing which records will—and which will not—be used again requires knowledge about the business and a fair amount of judgment.

TRANSFER. As records become inactive—referred to only infrequently— they should be culled from the files to make room for active records. Besides occupying valuable office space and equipment, inactive records get in the way of the efficient use of active ones. Periodically, then, infrequently used records should be removed from the main files and placed in *transfer files*. Transfer files look somewhat like regular files, except that the containers are less expensive (usually pressboard containers), and they are kept in less accessible locations, such as the basement, where floor space is less expensive than in the main office.

DISPOSAL. The last stage in the records management cycle is the disposal of records. Of course, all records that no longer serve a useful purpose should be destroyed. The decision as to when records are to be destroyed is usually made by management. The policy is determined by legal consid-erations and by the special needs of the business. At any rate some definite plan should be set up by management for the periodic destruction of records that are no longer of value to the organization.

FREEDOM OF INFORMATION ACT AND PRIVACY ACT

The use of computers to process and store information, much of which is personal in nature, has created concern that the information may be released to individuals or firms and used for reasons other than those for which it was originally intended. If the information is incorrect, that compounds the problem. For example, an error in a record of a person's account at a bank or department store may prove an obstacle to that person's ability to obtain credit elsewhere, if that record is released. It is conceivable that this error could even cause a collection agency to locate the individual's place of employment and have the person's wages garnished for a debt that doesn't exist.

In the fall of 1974, the United States Congress passed two laws to protect the individual against misuse of information on file. These laws affect the work done by the file worker in some situations. One of these laws is called the Freedom of Information Act. This law affects individuals and gives them the right to ask for information that pertains to them.

Records which might be requested include those kept in doctors' offices, hospitals, dental clinics, psychiatric offices, and even educational institutions. Records of lawyers, government agencies that have files about you, counselors, priests, lending institutions, and employment application files are all available to you to read when you obtain permission from the organization maintaining those records.

The other law which was passed at the same time was called the Privacy Act. This law controls information which is readily available to the public. It serves to safeguard individual privacy. For someone to see your records within a particular organization, your permission would be necessary.

Hence we can say that the Freedom of Information Act allows you to see records about yourself. The Privacy Act limits those people who are allowed to see information contained in files about you.

What does this mean to the file worker? It means that you may be responsible for files that are covered by the Acts. You might have to screen people who request access to the files. You might be in charge of checking permission granted to people to use the files. It might be your job also to see to it that persons requesting various files sign a logbook before they are allowed to see the files. You might also have the authority to refuse access to certain records and documents. Because of these responsibilities, you might have to qualify for a security classification in order to work for a government agency.

In addition to the laws which control access to the files, some businesses have files which they have determined contain confidential or secret information. These files are to be read and used only by those employees who have the "need to know" because their job duties require working with this information. Charge-out systems for these files are strict and rigidly enforced. In most cases the files cannot be removed beyond a specified area after being checked out, and no copies may be made of the contents. The employee requesting the confidential or secret file must present proper identification or authorization to the file worker or the worker must deny access.

OFFICE EMPLOYMENT AND FILING

Because records are so important in any organization, they influence, in some way, the activities of every employee. Those who work in the office are especially concerned with records—creating them and later finding and using them.

For most office workers, handling records is one of a number of job responsibilities. The secretarial position is an example of one that calls for filing and records management skills. The secretary is usually responsible for maintaining the employer's files and may in a small organization even have to set up a filing system for the organization or reorganize an existing system. The employer depends upon the secretary to find important information quickly. "Please get me a copy of the letter we wrote to the Centerville Brick Company about the building materials for the new lab" is a typical request made of a secretary. No secretary should consider secretarial training complete without a thorough knowledge of filing and records management procedures.

Courtesy Hewlett-Packard Co.

No matter what kind of office job you hold, you will have to work with records.

Other office workers also make use of office records. Typists, accountants, stenographers, word processing specialists, computer operators, and general clerical workers use files frequently. Although these workers may not be directly involved in filing activities, their effectiveness is increased if they understand the importance of systematic filing.

An office with centralized files may employ workers for full-time filing positions. Files are often kept in central locations, especially in larger organizations, because the centralization eliminates the need for duplication of records in separate department files. From these central locations, records can be easily obtained by all departments that may need them for reference purposes. The specialized file worker is an important person in the operation of the office. Positions as file supervisors exist also, to manage the filing department. Opportunities for advancement are excellent for those who have supervisory ability and wish to assume responsibilities.

The office manager should be well enough informed about filing techniques and records administration to be able to determine such matters as the type of filing system to be used, the equipment to be purchased, and the personnel needed to maintain the files.

CAREERS IN FILING

As you study filing systems and records management you may decide that you would like to specialize in this area of office management.

The *Dictionary of Occupational Titles* describes file clerks as individuals "concerned with classifying, sorting, and filing correspondence, records, and other data."[1] While this general category is broken down into many job titles and descriptions, the ones which follow will give you a general idea of the duties and responsibilities of each.

206.362-010 FILE CLERK (clerical) I

Files correspondence, cards, invoices, receipts, and other records in alphabetical or numerical order, or according to subject matter, phonetic spelling, or other system: Reads incoming material and sorts according to file system. Places material in file cabinet, drawers, boxes, or in special filing cases. Locates and removes material from files when requested. Keeps records of material removed, stamps material received, traces missing file folders, and types indexing information on folders. May enter data on records.

206.367-014 FILE CLERK (clerical) II

Performs duties essentially same as those of FILE CLERK (clerical) I, except that in addition to putting material in and removing it from files, performs clerical work in searching and investigating information contained in files, inserting additional data on file records, making up reports, and keeping files current, which may require making calculations, and supplying written information from file data. Classifies material when classification is not readily discernible. Disposes of obsolete files in accordance with established retirement schedule or legal requirements. May operate keypunch to enter data on

[1]*Dictionary of Occupational Titles,* 4th ed., U.S. Department of Labor, Employment and Training Administration, Washington, 1977, p. 158.

tabulating cards. May photograph records on microfilming devices. May type reports. May use calculating machine.

206.387-010 CLASSIFICATION CLERK (clerical) coding file clerk.

Classifies materials according to subject matter and assigns numbers or symbols from predetermined coding system to facilitate accurate filing and reference: Scans correspondence, reports, drawings, and other materials to be filed to determine subject matter. Ascertains specified number or symbol, using code book or chart, and marks or stamps code on material. Assigns cross-indexing numbers if subject matter should be classified and filed under more than one heading. May revise coding system to improve code usage.

206.137-010 SUPERVISOR, FILES (clerical) records-section supervisor.

Supervises and coordinates activities of workers engaged in maintaining central records files: Directs and assists workers in searching files to retrieve lost or missing records, utilizing knowledge of common filing errors. Routes incorrectly pulled files to workers for refiling. Directs and assists workers in periodic disposal of obsolete files, according to company policy and legal requirements. Directs and participates in special file studies as directed by management. May recommend changes in work procedures to improve filing-system efficiency.

In addition to records specialists and supervisors, many large businesses and organizations employ one or more records managers. These individuals usually have a four-year college degree and work as part of the management structure in the business. Their job duties may include:

1. Analysis, creation, and coordination of business forms.
2. Analysis, creation, and evaluation of records systems, including filing systems.
3. Planning and implementing micrographic systems.
4. Using the principles and techniques of records management to meet the needs of management.

The outlook for filing careers is, like that for most office occupations, very good. The current *Occupational Outlook Handbook* will give you up-to-date information about the nature of the work, places of employment, training, and other qualifications, advancement, employment outlook, and earning and working conditions. Currently there are more than a quarter of a million persons employed as file workers. This position can often be held on a part-time basis and is often an entry-level job leading to advancement. Because of business expansion and growing amounts of paperwork, opportunities for employment are plentiful in filing careers.[2]

Records managers and other individuals who deal with records and information management may be members of the Association of Records Managers and Administrators, Inc. (ARMA). This is a nonprofit organiza-

[2]*Occupational Outlook Handbook, 1978–1979,* U.S. Department of Labor, Bureau of Labor Statistics, Bulletin 1955, Washington, 1978, pp. 95–97.

tion to provide guidance and to promote interest, research, and the exchange of ideas concerning records and information management. Many communities have local chapters whose members meet regularly to discuss topics and problems of current interest.

SURVEY OF COMPETENCIES

GENERAL REVIEW

The following questions will help you to reinforce your learning of the competencies included in this chapter.

1. Why is filing and records management important to you as an individual? (Competency 1)
2. Define the following terms. (Competencies 2, 5)

   caption   procedure
   correspondence   records
   filing   records management
   filing system   system
   method
3. Why are business records necessary? Name three records that businesses and individuals need to keep. (Competency 3)
4. What are the two basic methods used for filing? (Competency 4)
5. What are the four classifications businesses use to value their records? Give two examples of records for each classification. (Competency 6)
6. List and briefly describe the stages in the life cycle of a business record. (Competency 7)
7. What is the Freedom of Information Act? What is the Privacy Act? How are these two acts different? Why is each important in filing? (Competency 8)
8. What is meant by the "need to know"? Why is this important to you as a file worker? (Competency 9)
9. Why do office employees need to have a knowledge of filing? (Competency 10)
10. Name five job titles in filing and records management. List two job duties of each. (Competency 11)

CASE PROBLEMS

1. John Williams owns a service station. He told a friend of his, Ted Martin, that he does not need to keep an organized set of records. Ted said that John should keep well-planned files. With whom do you agree? Why? (Competencies 3, 6, 7)
2. Irene Jorgensen, who is employed as a file worker in a large insurance company, told a co-worker that the keeping of records is more important in a large organization than it is in a small one. Her co-worker disagrees. Who is right? Why? (Competencies 3, 6, 7)

3. Upon graduation from college, Frieda Webber expects to work in her uncle's large real estate office. She says that she does not plan to take a course in records management because it will not be useful in her job. Do you agree or disagree with her? Why? (Competencies 1, 3, 10)
4. You work for a man who dislikes keeping anything unless it is absolutely necessary. Samuel Jackson's motto is, "If in doubt, throw it out." You believe that motto should be, "If in doubt, keep it," when it comes to filing correspondence and business records. Who is right? Why? (Competencies 6, 7)
5. Your Aunt Louise has been encouraging you to apply for a part-time job in the filing department of the company for which she works. You want a career as a secretary or administrative assistant, and you feel that working as a records specialist will hurt your chances to be considered for another job. Should you apply for the job as a file worker? (Competencies 1, 10)
6. Marvin Brown works in the personnel department of a large company. He needs to refer to employees' files from time to time. He resents the fact that the file worker who controls those files asks for his authorization to see the information he needs. He feels that under the FOIA he has a right to see those files. Is he correct? (Competencies 8, 9)
7. When you began your program of studies, you were surprised to find that you would have a course in filing and records management. You have been wondering why filing is so important that you must spend that much time learning about it. What have you learned in this chapter to convince you that filing and records management is necessary to your career as an office employee? (Competencies 1, 3, 10, 11)

If you have not mastered all of the competencies reviewed in the Survey, reread that part of the chapter which deals with the competency in question; then recheck your progress.

Alphabetic Indexing: Individual Names

COMPETENCIES

When you have completed this chapter, you will be able to:

1. Define the terms *alphabetizing, indexing, caption,* and *unit.*
2. Type or write names of individuals in indexing order on cards. Alphabetize, file, and find the cards. (See Jobs 1 to 5 in the *Practice Materials* and Exercises 1 to 5 in the Appendix.)
3. Prepare alphabetic cross-reference cards containing names of individuals, and arrange them in sequence with alphabetic cards. (See Jobs 4 and 5 in the *Practice Materials* or Exercises 4 and 5 in the Appendix.)

TERMINOLOGY

The process of putting names or items in alphabetic order according to the sequence of their letters is called *alphabetizing.* Many things with which you are already familiar, such as the telephone book and the card catalog in the library, use the principle of alphabetizing. In the business world, this is the logical way to organize much of the information used in day-to-day business operations.

When putting names in alphabetic order, you begin by looking at the first letter of each name. For example, you would file the names *Addison, Baker, Carter,* and *Douglas* according to *A, B, C, D.* If the first letters are identical, as in the names *James, Johnson, Jones, Joyner,* and *Joynes,* you need to compare second, third, and even last letters to determine which name should come first.

Indexing is the process of deciding which name to file a record under and then deciding the proper order of the words in that name. The filing term for the name a paper is filed under is *caption.* (Sometimes the word *heading* is used to mean the same as *caption.*) Each part of the caption that is used for filing purposes is called a *unit.* Suppose you had the name *Richard G. Stone* to file. The caption is *Richard G. Stone;* the units, three in this case, are *Richard, G.,* and *Stone.*

RULES FOR ALPHABETIC INDEXING

There are twenty-five rules for alphabetic indexing. These rules are organized into three groups: rules that apply to names of individuals; rules that apply to names of business firms; and rules that apply to special organizations such as educational institutions, hotels and motels, and government bodies. This chapter presents the eight rules that apply to names of individuals.

RULE 1. ALPHABETIC ORDER

Alphabetize names by comparing the first units of the names letter by letter. Consider second units only when the first units are identical. Consider third units only when both the first and second units are identical, and so on.

Note: If two names are identical, consider addresses. (See Rule 18.)

NAME	UNIT 1	UNIT 2	UNIT 3
Andrews	Andrews		
Barnes	Barnes		
Bennett	Bennett		
Carson Dress Shop	Carson	Dress	Shop
Carson Shoe Place	Carson	Shoe	Place
Carson Shoe Store	Carson	Shoe	Store

Can You Apply the Rule?

In each of the following groups, which name will be filed first and why?

1. Berg   Burg
2. Noonan   Michaels
3. Roberts Auto Shop   Roberts Auto Store

Turn to page 26 to check your answers.

RULE 2. NOTHING COMES BEFORE SOMETHING

A name consisting of a single letter comes before a name consisting of a word that begins with the same letter. A name consisting of one word comes before a name that consists of the same word plus one or more other words. A name consisting of two or more words comes before a name that consists of the same two or more words plus another word, and so on.

NAME	UNIT 1	UNIT 2	UNIT 3
B	B		
Baker	Baker		
Baker Warehouse	Baker	Warehouse	
Baker Warehouse Storage	Baker	Warehouse	Storage

Can You Apply the Rule?

In each of the following groups, which name will be filed first and why?

1. Z Store   Zebra Store
2. Samuel Dry Goods   Samuels
3. A Auto   A Auto School

Turn to page 26 to check your answers.

RULE 3. LAST NAME FIRST

Treat each part of the name of an individual as a separate unit, and consider the units in this order: last name (surname), first name (given name) or initial, middle name or initial (if any).

NAME	UNIT 1	UNIT 2	UNIT 3
C. H. Anderson	Anderson	C.	H.
Harry J. Brown	Brown	Harry	J.
William Brown	Brown	William	
L. George Clark	Clark	L.	George
Lee S. Clark	Clark	Lee	S.
Leigh A. Clark	Clark	Leigh	A.

Can You Apply the Rule?

In each of the following groups, which name will be filed first and why?

1. Dawn Parker   D. M. Parker
2. David R. Stanley   David C. Stanley
3. Roberta Welch   Roberta Wells

Turn to page 26 to check your answers.

TYPING NAMES FOR CARD FILING

Now that you have learned the first three rules for filing individual names, you need to know how to type the names on file cards.

Using a standard format for typing on cards makes the job of filing easier since the information will be located in exactly the same place on each card. In addition, it creates a uniform and businesslike appearance.

Follow these steps for proper format and style for typing names on file cards:

1. Type the parts of the name in indexing order. For example, the name *John T. Smith* would be typed *Smith, John T.*
2. Begin typing the name three spaces from the left edge of the card on the second line from the top.
3. You may type the name in all-capital letters, *SMITH, JOHN T.,* or you may type it with initial caps, *Smith, John T.* You should be consistent in following whichever style is preferred in your office.
4. Usually normal punctuation is used; however, punctuation may be omitted with two spaces left where it would have been. *(Smith, J. Thomas* or *Smith   J   Thomas)* Again, be consistent in following the style preferred by your office.
5. Copy the name of the company or individual exactly as it is used by that person or company. For example, *Baker & Sons* would be typed using the ampersand (&), not the word *and*. *Michael d'Angelo* would be typed with a small *d* instead of a capital letter. *Van Doren* would be typed with a space between *Van* and *Doren*.
6. If your office chooses to abbreviate common words such as *Company* and *Incorporated* to save time when typing cards, some indication such as an asterisk (*) following the abbreviated word should be used to indicate that the business prefers the word spelled out.

━━━━━━━━━━━━━ **TYPING PRACTICE** ━━━━━━━━━━━━━

Complete the typing practice in the *Practice Materials* or complete Exercise 1 in the Appendix, page 191.

ROUGH AND FINE SORTING TECHNIQUES

When you are working with cards or papers that need to be filed, sort them into alphabetic order before storing them. If you have a great number of papers to sort, sort first into a range of letters, such as all papers to be filed under *A-H.* Then sort again by individual letter. The first sorting is *rough sorting;* the second is *fine sorting.* Using rough and fine sorting is helpful because it saves time and helps prevent mistakes in filing. Sort papers on a desk top or another surface large enough to hold several piles of papers.

Follow these steps for rough and fine sorting:

1. Sort the cards into four general divisions of the alphabet such as *A-F, G-M, N-T, U-Z.* When doing your exercises, since you will not be working with the entire alphabet, use *P, Q, R, S, T,* and *U* as your divisions.
2. Fine sorting consists of putting each pile into alphabetic order. After the first group is sorted, place it face down. As each successive group is sorted, place it face down on top of the preceding one. When you are done, you should have all the items in correct order. (If you are working with a large number of items, you will need to sort each of your first four groups into four additional groups as many times as necessary to achieve a workable number of cards to put into exact alphabetic order.)

━━━━━━━━━━ FILING PRACTICE ━━━━━━━━━━

You are now ready to complete Job 1 of the *Practice Materials.* If the *Practice Materials* are not available, complete Exercise 1 on page 191 of the Appendix.

RULE 4. PREFIXES

Consider a prefix (such as *Mc* in *McDonald*) as part of the name, not as a separate unit. Ignore variations in spacing, punctuation, or capitalization in names that contain prefixes (for example, *d', D', Da, de, De, Del, Des, Di, Du, Fitz, La, Le, M', Mac, O', St., Van, Van de, Van der, Von,* and *Von der*).

Note: Consider the prefixes *M', Mac,* and *Mc* exactly as they are spelled.

Note: Alphabetize the prefix *St.* as though it were spelled *Saint.*

NAME	UNIT 1	UNIT 2	UNIT 3
John A. D'Angelo	D'Angelo	John	A.
John C. De Angelo	De Angelo	John	C.
John R. Deangelo	Deangelo	John	R.
Jean MacIntosh	MacIntosh	Jean	
Curtis McCarty	McCarty	Curtis	
Sally O'Hara	O'Hara	Sally	
James T. St. Clair	St. Clair	James	T.
Robert VanDerkamp	VanDerkamp	Robert	
Helen E. Van Nortwick	Van Nortwick	Helen	E.

The illustration on page 17 shows names in Rule 4 typed and filed in proper sequence.

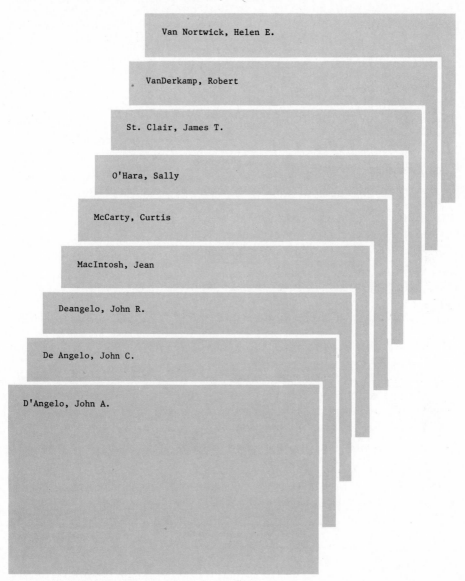

Van Nortwick, Helen E.

VanDerkamp, Robert

St. Clair, James T.

O'Hara, Sally

McCarty, Curtis

MacIntosh, Jean

Deangelo, John R.

De Angelo, John C.

D'Angelo, John A.

Can You Apply the Rule?

In each of the following groups, which name will be filed first and why?

1. Mary Saintjohn   Mary S. St. John
2. D'Eramo   DeRamo
3. MacMillan   McLellan

Turn to page 26 to check your answers.

RULE 5. HYPHENATED INDIVIDUAL NAMES

Consider a hyphenated part of an individual's name as *one* indexing unit. Ignore the hyphen.

NAME	UNIT 1	UNIT 2	UNIT 3
John Eric-Williams	Eric-Williams	John	
Ann-Marie Reed	Reed	Ann-Marie	
Arthur Maxwell Reed	Reed	Arthur	Maxwell
Nancy R. Spencer-Harris	Spencer-Harris	Nancy	R.

Can You Apply the Rule?

In each of the following groups, which name will be filed first and why?

1. Mary-Ann Davis   Mary Ann Davis
2. Jane Ferris Hansen   Jane Ferris-Hansen
3. Steve Ludwig   Martha Goldstein-Ludwig

Turn to page 26 to check your answers.

▬▬▬▬ FILING PRACTICE ▬▬▬▬

Complete Job 2 of the *Practice Materials*. If the *Practice Materials* are not available, complete Exercise 2 on page 192 of the Appendix.

RULE 6. TITLES

Ignore a title used with the last name plus one or more other parts of an individual's name, but consider a title as the first unit if it is used with only one part of an individual's name.

Note: Consider the title *Mrs.* if a woman uses her husband's name and you do not know her first name. Treat *Mrs.* as it is spelled.

NAME	UNIT 1	UNIT 2	UNIT 3
Captain Daniels	Captain	Daniels	
Captain Ronald Daniels	Daniels	Ronald	
Congressman R. T. Smith	Smith	R.	T.
Mr. Andrew Snyder	Snyder	Andrew	
Mrs. Andrew Snyder (whose first name is not known)	Snyder	Andrew	Mrs.
Mrs. Andrew Snyder (whose first name is Cora)	Snyder	Cora	

Can You Apply the Rule?

In each of the following groups, which name will be filed first and why?

1. Commander Frost   Commander William Frost
2. Mrs. Leo Kaplan (Lynne)   Mrs. Leo Kaplan (first name is not
known)
3. Captain Barney   Barbara Captain

Turn to page 26 to check your answers.

RULE 7. SENIORITY TERMS AND OTHER DESIGNATIONS FOLLOWING THE NAME

Ignore a seniority term (such as *Sr., Jr., II,* and *III*), a professional degree (such as *CPA, M.D.,* and *Ph.D.*), or any other designation following a name.

Note: When indexing two names that are identical, see Rule 18.

NAME	UNIT 1	UNIT 2	UNIT 3
Dennis Katz, D.D.S., P.C.*	Katz	Dennis	
Dr. John L. Marshall, Jr.	Marshall	John	L.
Donald Waddell, Jr.	Waddell	Donald	
Donald R. Waddell, III	Waddell	Donald	R.

*Private Corporation, often used by professional individuals in business for themselves.

Can You Apply the Rule?

In each of the following groups, which name will be filed first and why?

1. Clyde D. Newton, Jr.   Clyde Newton, Sr.
2. Wilbur Little, D.D.S.   Mr. Wilburn Little, CPA
3. Eleanor Backman, R.N.   Eleanor Bachman, Ed.D.

Turn to pages 26 and 27 to check your answers.

RULE 8. ABBREVIATED NAMES AND NICKNAMES

Consider any abbreviated part of a name (such as *Chas.* for *Charles*) as though it were written in full.

Consider a name such as *Bob* for *Robert* or *Liz* for *Elizabeth* only if it is the true name rather than a nickname or if the true name is not known.

NAME	UNIT 1	UNIT 2	UNIT 3
John (Johnny) Battin	Battin	John	
Geo. M. Leonard	Leonard	George	M.
Billy K. Rogers	Rogers	Billy	K.
William L. Rogers (Billy)	Rogers	William	L.
Patricia V. Stevens (Tricia)	Stevens	Patricia	V.
Patrick A. Stevens (Pat)	Stevens	Patrick	A.

Can You Apply the Rule?

In each of the following groups, which name will be filed first and why?

1. "Bud" Lockwood (Walter)   Walter B. Lockwood ("Bud")
2. Nan Paterson (Nannette)   Nancy Patterson
3. "Red" Maguire (given name unknown)   "Red" Maguire (Kevin, Jr.)

Turn to page 27 to check your answers.

FILING PRACTICE

Complete Job 3 of the *Practice Materials*. If the *Practice Materials* are not available, complete Exercise 3 on page 192 of the Appendix.

CROSS-REFERENCING INDIVIDUAL NAMES

A record should always be filed under the caption by which it is most likely to be requested. When some records may be requested under more than one caption, it is then necessary to cross-reference the records under the alternate captions.

Cross-referencing for individuals may be necessary in the following circumstances:

1. When it is difficult to tell which unit is the individual's last name and which is the first name.

FILED UNDER	CROSS-REFERENCE
Frank, Nelson	Nelson, Frank
Lee, Brooke	Brooke, Lee
Nam, Ling	Ling, Nam

2. When an individual has a name change as in the case of marriage, divorce, or adoption. The cross-reference will be necessary only until all records appear in the new name and reference to the former name is no longer necessary.

FILED UNDER	CROSS-REFERENCE	REASON
Hobson, Willette Ferguson	'Ferguson, Willette	Marriage
Shepard, Amy	Kelly, Amy Shepard	Divorce, return to maiden name
Kerr, Marjorie	Rice, Marjorie	Adoption by stepfather

3. When an individual uses one name for professional purposes and a different one for legal or social purposes. Examples are a stage name

and the name of a professional woman who has earned her credentials under one name and has since been married or divorced.

FILED UNDER	CROSS-REFERENCE	REASON
Clark, Victoria (M.D.)	Fisher, Victoria (Mrs. Earl)	Married, uses professional name for business purposes
Janowski, Joseph Gregory	January, Joe	Professional stage name

4. When records of two or more individuals need to be kept in the same file. Examples are medical records for members of a family, apartment lease records for college students, and cochairpersons of a committee.

FILED UNDER	CROSS-REFERENCE	REASON
Kerr, Ralph	Kerr, Marjorie	Medical records for members of the same family
Martin, Peter	Johnson, Carol Kensington, Mark	Cosigners on a lease
Townsend, Barbara	Gilbert, Jacob	Cochairpersons

The illustration on page 22 shows alphabetic name and cross-reference cards typed and filed in proper sequence.

Can You Cross-Reference Individual Names?

Indicate the file and cross-reference captions for each of the following names:

1. An Wong
2. Michael David
3. Irene O'Conner marries Stuart Brooks.
4. Andrew Fitzpatrick adopts Sheila Morrison.
5. Lamonte Worthington, an actor, uses the stage name Larry Lamonte.
6. Angela Ridgeway, a practicing attorney you deal with professionally, marries Grant Haber.
7. Dorothy Miller, Carol Pryor, and Adrienne Wilson lease an apartment together.
8. Laura Underwood's high school records will remain filed under her maiden name, Laura Smith, but a cross-reference card will be prepared to show her new name.

Turn to page 27 to check your answers.

ALPHABETIC NAME AND CROSS-REFERENCE CARDS
CORRECTLY TYPED AND FILED IN PROPER SEQUENCE.

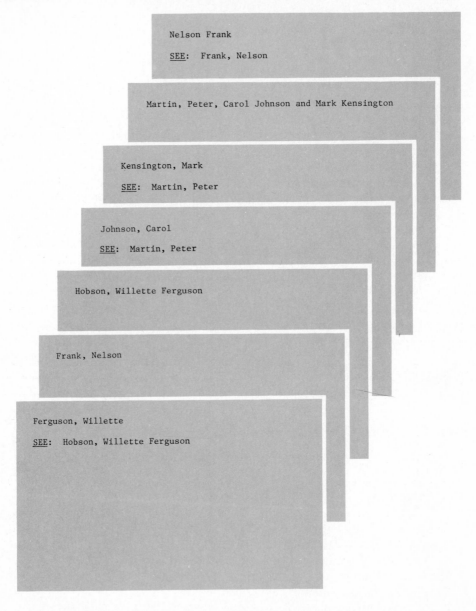

Nelson Frank

SEE: Frank, Nelson

Martin, Peter, Carol Johnson and Mark Kensington

Kensington, Mark

SEE: Martin, Peter

Johnson, Carol

SEE: Martin, Peter

Hobson, Willette Ferguson

Frank, Nelson

Ferguson, Willette

SEE: Hobson, Willette Ferguson

━━━━━━━━━━ FILING PRACTICE ━━━━━━━━━━

Complete Jobs 4 and 5 of the *Practice Materials*. If the *Practice Materials* are not available, complete Exercises 4 and 5 on pages 192–193 of the Appendix.

SURVEY OF COMPETENCIES

GENERAL REVIEW

You have had an opportunity to put into practice much of the material you have learned in this chapter. There are a few points, however, that you need to review to reinforce your learning of these concepts.

1. Define the following terms:
   a. alphabetizing
   b. indexing
   c. caption
   d. unit
   (Competency 1)
2. Using the names given in the *Practice Materials* or in the exercises in the Appendix, demonstrate how names should be typed on index and cross-reference cards. Following your instructor's directions, you may state orally or in writing or type to illustrate the proper method. (Competencies 2, 3)
3. Using the cards contained in the *Practice Materials,* or index and cross-reference cards on which you have typed or written the names in the exercises in the Appendix, demonstrate the correct rough and fine sorting techniques for putting cards in alphabetic order. If you do not have these materials available, list orally or in writing the steps you should follow. (Competencies 2, 3)

You practiced Competencies 2 and 3 in the *Practice Materials* or Appendix exercises. The following indexing review will reinforce your ability to select indexing units.

INDEXING REVIEW

A. What is the *first* indexing unit of each of the following names?

1. R. L. Smith	6. Smith, Robert L.
2. R. L. Benson-Smith	7. Robert L. Smith, Jr.
3. Mr. Benson Smith	8. Doctor Smith
4. Mrs. Benson Smith (Shirley)	9. Dr. Robert L. Smith
5. Shirley-Anne Benson	10. Shirley A. Smith, Ph.D.

B. What is the *second* indexing unit of each of the following names?

1. K. T. Johnson	6. Nancy Johnson-Sutherland
2. Mrs. K. T. Johnson (Rachel)	7. K. T. Johnson, III
3. Mr. "Bud" Johnson (Kenneth)	8. Chas. Johnson
4. Nancy-Lee Johnson	9. Martin Johnson Van Camp
5. Nurse Johnson	10. "Butch" Johnson (first name unknown)

C. What is the *third* indexing unit of each of the following names? (If there is no third indexing unit, the correct answer is *none*.)

1. Larry MacQuillan, Jr.
2. Mr. John T. Cooper
3. Mrs. John T. Cooper (Cora)
4. Sara F. Schultz (Mrs. Jason R.)
5. John R. Shoemaker, M.D.
6. Marvin St. James
7. Nancy-Lee Andrews-Turner
8. Ted M. Turner (Theodore)
9. Barbie Knight (Barbara D.)
10. Amelia Renee O'Keefe

D. Alphabetize the names in each of the following groups. On a separate sheet of paper, list the letters to indicate the correct alphabetic order.

1. a. Caroline Young
   b. C. Young
   c. Carolyn Young
2. a. Pamela York
   b. Mike York (Michael)
   c. Mr. Mike C. York
3. a. Donovan
   b. Major Timothy F. Donovan, Jr.
   c. Tim (Timothy) Donovan
4. a. J. Norcross
   b. R. Mercer
   c. G. O'Hearn
5. a. Marvin O'Neill
   b. Marv O'Neal (first name unknown)
   c. Mrs. Marvin O'Neal, Sr. (Mamie)
6. a. Arthur Gray
   b. Gilbert Hackett
   c. Glenna Gray-Hackett
7. a. Mary-Ellen Winslow
   b. Mary Ellen Winslow
   c. Mary Ellen-Winslow
8. a. Doctor Bill
   b. Dr. Bill Perkins (Robert William)
   c. Dr. Bill Perkins (William)
9. a. Lt. Benjamin Reid, Jr.
   b. Col. Ben S. Reid, Sr. (Benjamin)
   c. Benjamin Reed
10. a. Morris Cook
    b. Mister Cook
    c. Mrs. Belinda Cook

CASE PROBLEMS

1. You are employed by a small business which has the files set up in alphabetic order according to the names of the customers. One of them, Janet Burgess, was recently married to Arnold McLellan. When you wanted to file a letter from Janet McLellan, referring to a previous transaction, you could not find a folder for her. There was no indication in the folder for Arnold McLellan that she was married to him. Before her marriage, Janet had notified the office of her name change and requested a new charge account plate with the name *Mrs. Janet McLellan* and the same account number as her husband. She also requested that her present account be canceled. This letter was stored in the folder with the caption *Burgess, Janet.* (a) What had not been done that should have been done? (b) What steps can you take to find her file? (c) When you do find Janet's file, what will you do to avoid this problem in the future? (Competency 3)

2. You keep a file of the names and addresses of your clients. The cards have been typed as shown below:
   (a) What is wrong with this system? (b) What should be done in the future as new cards are typed?   (Competency 2)

```
Jones, James L.
99 Terrace Road
Rochester, NY 14624
```

```
LAMAR   GRACE N
203 MEADOW LANE
ROCHESTER   NEW YORK 14618
```

```
MARCHACK, Eugene Frank, 1206 Burgundy Street,
   Rochester, NY 14624
```

3. As part of your daily job routine, you have been asked to file cards in their proper locations. File drawers are set up with alphabetic ranges as guide captions, with some alphabet letters taking up two or three drawers. You are given stacks of 100 or more cards to file at a time. What is a more efficient method for you to store the cards than to take the stack as given to you, pick up each card one at a time, and place it in the proper drawer? Describe the steps you would follow.   (Competency 2)

If you have not mastered all of the competencies reviewed in the Survey, reread that part of the chapter which deals with the competency in question; then recheck your progress.

RULE 1
1. **Berg** comes before **Bu**rg; you need to watch closely for variations in the spelling of similar names.
2. Michaels comes before **N**oonan; *M* comes before *N* in the alphabet.
3. Roberts Auto **Sh**op comes before Roberts Auto **St**ore; the first two units are the same and so the third unit determines the sequence.

RULE 2
1. **Z** Store comes before **Z**ebra Store; the letter *Z* comes before a word which begins with *Z*.
2. **Samuel** Dry Goods comes before **Samuels;** in this case, only the first units need to be compared, and they are identical except for the letter *s*.
3. **A Auto** comes before **A Auto S**chool; nothing comes before something.

RULE 3
1. **D.** M. Parker comes before **Dawn** Parker; the second indexing units determine the order.
2. David **C.** Stanley comes before David **R.** Stanley; the third indexing units determine the order.
3. Roberta Wel**ch** comes before Roberta Wel**ls**; the first indexing units determine the order.

RULE 4
1. **Mary** Saintjohn comes before **Mary S.** St. John; the first and second indexing units are identical so you need to consider the third unit, and nothing comes before something.
2. Either **D'Er**amo or **DeR**amo may be first; the units are identical for indexing purposes.
3. **Mac**Millan comes before **Mc**Lellan.

RULE 5
1. **Mary** Ann Davis comes before **Mary-A**nn Davis; nothing comes before something in the second units *Mary* and *Mary-Ann*.
2. Jane Ferris-Hansen comes before Jane Ferris Hansen.
3. Martha Goldstein-Ludwig comes before Steve Ludwig.

RULE 6
1. Commander Frost comes before William **F**rost; the first units are *Commander* and *Frost;* the title in the second name is disregarded.
2. Mrs. **Leo** Kaplan comes before **Lynne** Kaplan; did you remember to use the married woman's given name as the second unit?
3. **Barb**ara Captain comes before Captain **Barn**ey; the first units are both *Captain* since *Captain Barney* is a title with only part of an individual's name.

RULE 7
1. **Clyde** Newton comes before **Clyde D.** Newton; the seniority titles are disregarded, and nothing comes before something.

2. **Wilbur** Little comes before **Wilburn** Little; notice the difference in the spelling of the first names.

3. Eleanor **Bach**man comes before Eleanor **Back**man; the titles are disregarded. It is important to check similar spellings of names carefully, especially when the pronunciation may be the same.

RULE 8

1. **Walter** Lockwood comes before **Walter B.** Lockwood; the nicknames have no effect on the filing sequence.

2. Nannette **Pater**son comes before Nancy **Patt**erson; the last names are spelled differently.

3. Kevin Maguire comes before "**Red**" Maguire; when a given name is unknown, the nickname is used as an indexing unit.

CROSS-REFERENCING INDIVIDUAL NAMES

FILED UNDER	CROSS-REFERENCE
Wong, An	An, Wong
David, Michael	Michael, David
Brooks, Irene O'Conner	O'Conner, Irene
Fitzpatrick, Sheila	Morrison, Sheila
Worthington, Lamonte	Lamonte, Larry
Ridgeway, Angela	Haber, Angela Ridgeway (Mrs. Grant)
Miller, Dorothy	Pryor, Carol
	Wilson, Adrienne
Smith, Laura	Underwood, Laura

3
Alphabetic Indexing: Business and Special Names

COMPETENCIES

When you have completed this chapter, you will be able to:

1. Type or write business and special names in indexing order on cards. Alphabetize, file, and find the cards. (See Jobs 6 to 14 in the *Practice Materials*.)
2. Prepare alphabetic cross-reference cards containing business and special names and arrange them in sequence with alphabetic cards. (See Jobs 13 and 14 in the *Practice Materials*.)
3. Name instances when the cross-referencing of business and special names may be necessary.
4. State examples in which indexing rules might be varied or changed to meet the needs of special business situations.
5. Explain the purpose and necessity of filing rules.

This chapter presents the specific rules for indexing business and special names used in addition to the rules for individual names in Chapter 2. When you have completed your study of these rules and have done the related practice, you will have mastered the twenty-five rules in common usage to keep individual, business, and special names filed in an organized and consistent manner.

RULES FOR ALPHABETIC INDEXING

RULE 9. FIRST WORD FIRST

Treat each word in the name of a business firm as a separate unit, and consider the units in the same order as they are written.

Exception: When the name of a business firm includes the last name of an individual plus one or more of that person's other names, transpose only the parts of the individual's name (last name first—see Rule 3).

NAME	UNIT 1	UNIT 2	UNIT 3	UNIT 4
C. A. Clinton Company	Clinton	C.	A.	Company
Charles Clinton Company	Clinton	Charles	Company	
Clinton Construction Company	Clinton	Construction	Company	
Kensington Pharmacy	Kensington	Pharmacy		
Bonnie Kerns Learning Center	Kerns	Bonnie	Learning	Center

Note: Consider a title in a firm name as an indexing unit. Treat abbreviated titles as though they were written in full, except *Mr., Mrs.,* and *Ms.*

NAME	UNIT 1	UNIT 2	UNIT 3	UNIT 4
Coach Dan Sporting Goods	Coach	Dan	Sporting	Goods
Mr. Seafood Fish Factory	Mr.	Seafood	Fish	Factory
Mrs. Owens Bakery	Mrs.	Owens	Bakery	

Can You Apply the Rule?

In each of the following groups, which name will be filed first and why?

1. Mr. Big Restaurant   Raymond Bigelow Imports
2. Mrs. Plants Flowers   Plant House Flowers
3. University Auto Leasing   University Automobile Leasing

Turn to pages 45 and 46 to check your answers.

RULE 10. ARTICLES, CONJUNCTIONS, AND PREPOSITIONS

Ignore an article, conjunction, or preposition (such as *a, an, and, &, for, in, of,* or *the*) in the name of a business firm unless it is a distinctive part of the name. Consider foreign articles such as *El, La, Le, Les,* and *Los* and noncontemporary words such as *Thee, Thy,* and *Ye* as indexing units.

NAME	UNIT 1	UNIT 2	UNIT 3	UNIT 4
Clocks of Yesterday	Clocks	Yesterday		
La Boutique	La	Boutique		
The Paul Miller Company	Miller	Paul	Company	
Ye Olde Clock Shoppe	Ye	Olde	Clock	Shoppe

Can You Apply the Rule?

In each of the following groups, which name will be filed first and why?

1. El Patio Restaurant   Patio and Restaurant Shop
2. A Pet Shoppe   Pet Shop
3. Thy Leisure Reading Store   The Leisure Reading Store

Turn to page 46 to check your answers.

 **FILING PRACTICE**

Complete Job 6 of the *Practice Materials.* If the *Practice Materials* are not available, complete Exercise 6 on page 194 of the Appendix.

RULE 11. ABBREVIATIONS

Treat an abbreviated word in a firm name as though the word were written in full.

NAME	UNIT 1	UNIT 2	UNIT 3	UNIT 4
International Foods, Ltd.	International	Foods	Limited	
Jones Bros. Salvage Corp.	Jones	Brothers	Salvage	Corporation
Jas. Jones, Inc.	Jones	James	Incorporated	
Western Mfg. Co.	Western	Manufacturing	Company	

Can You Apply the Rule?

In each of the following groups, which name will be filed first and why?

1. Data Systems Mfg. Div.   Data Systems Manufacturers
2. O. M. Walker Co., Inc.   Walker Company, Inc.
3. Martin Brothers Co.   Brother Martin Company

Turn to page 46 to check your answers.

RULE 12. SINGLE LETTERS

Consider single letters that are not abbreviations as separate units, whether they are separated by spaces or not.

Note: Single letters that are hyphenated should be considered as one unit. (See Rule 13.)

NAME	UNIT 1	UNIT 2	UNIT 3	UNIT 4	UNIT 5	UNIT 6
N & L Office Supplies	N	L	Office	Supplies		
WWVA Television Station	W	W	V	A	Television	Station
X Y Z Electronics	X	Y	Z	Electronics		

Can You Apply the Rule?

In each of the following groups, which name will be filed first and why?

1. ABC Diaper Service   A B C Toy Store
2. Everything A to Z   A to Z Research Service
3. B J Gifts   Blue Jay Florist and Gifts

Turn to page 46 to check your answers.

RULE 13. HYPHENATED FIRM NAMES

Consider hyphenated parts of a firm name as one unit.

NAME	UNIT 1	UNIT 2	UNIT 3	UNIT 4
A-Z Rent-All	A-Z	Rent-All		
Lewis-McKenzie Dept. Store	Lewis-McKenzie	Department	Store	
Louis McKenzie Dept. Store	McKenzie	Louis	Department	Store
Phoenix Drive-In	Phoenix	Drive-In		

Can You Apply the Rule?

In each of the following groups, which name will be filed first and why?

1. Robert-Wade Jewelry Store   Robert Wade Hardware Store
2. Do-It-Yourself Shop   Do It Yourself Hobby Store
3. Manuel-Ramirez Co.   M-R Company

Turn to page 46 to check your answers.

RULE 14. ONE OR TWO WORDS

Consider as one unit a part of a firm name that may be written as one word, as two words, or with a hyphen.

NAME	UNIT 1	UNIT 2	UNIT 3
Aero-Space Company	Aero-Space	Company	
Aero Space, Inc.	Aero Space	Incorporated	
Hill Crest Drug Store	Hill Crest	Drug	Store
Hill-Crest Shoe Store	Hill-Crest	Shoe	Store
North-West Air Line	North-West	Air Line	
Northwest Airlines	Northwest	Airlines	
North West Amusement Park	North West	Amusement	Park

Can You Apply the Rule?

In each of the following groups, which name will be filed first and why?

1. Sea Coast Restaurant   Seacoast Gift Shop
2. Sky Pike Trucking Co.   Sky Line Boating Co.
3. Interlake Steamship Manufacturers   Inter Lake Steam Ship Company

Turn to page 46 to check your answers.

━━━━━━━━━━ FILING PRACTICE ━━━━━━━━━━

Complete Job 7 of the *Practice Materials*. If the *Practice Materials* are not available, complete Exercise 7 on page 194 of the Appendix.

RULE 15. POSSESSIVES AND CONTRACTIONS

Ignore the apostrophe and consider all letters in a possessive or a contraction.

NAME	UNIT 1	UNIT 2	UNIT 3	UNIT 4
Carl Anderson's Woodworking Shop	Anderson's	Carl	Woodworking	Shop
Don't Tarry Convenience Store	Don't	Tarry	Convenience	Store
Ellen's Needlecraft Boutique	Ellen's	Needlecraft	Boutique	
T J's Sub Shop	T	J's	Sub	Shop

Can You Apply the Rule?

In each of the following groups, which name will be filed first and why?

1. It's About Time Watch Repair   I. T.'s Hair Fashions
2. Hasting's Appliance Service   Hastings' Appliance Store
3. David's Photo Mart   Bob Davids' Photo Mart

Turn to pages 46 and 47 to check your answers.

RULE 16. NUMBERS

Consider a number in the name of a business firm as though it were written in words, and treat it as one unit. Express the number in as few words as possible. For example, treat *1,543* as *fifteen hundred forty-three*, not *one thousand five hundred forty-three*.

NAME	UNIT 1	UNIT 2	UNIT 3
A-1 Rental	A-One	Rental	
Cadet Troop 104	Cadet	Troop	One hundred four
8 to 5 Temporaries	Eight	Five	Temporaries
9th Street Cafe	Ninth	Street	Cafe
7 Cities Realty	Seven	Cities	Realty
1776 Gift Shop	Seventeen hundred seventy-six	Gift	Shop

Can You Apply the Rule?

In each of the following groups, which name will be filed first and why?

1. Four Seasons Nursery   4th Avenue Garage
2. 7-Day Repair Service   7 Rider Carpool Service
3. Apartment House 83   Apartment House 1883

Turn to page 47 to check your answers.

RULE 17. PARTS OF GEOGRAPHIC NAMES

Consider each part of a geographic name as a separate indexing unit.

Exception: Treat hyphenated parts of a geographic name as one unit.

NAME	UNIT 1	UNIT 2	UNIT 3	UNIT 4
Newport News Bottling Co.	Newport	News	Bottling	Company
Santa Monica Civic Assn.	Santa	Monica	Civic	Association
South Carolina Construction Co.	South	Carolina	Construction	Company
Truckee River Inn	Truckee	River	Inn	
Winston-Salem Paper Company	Winston-Salem	Paper	Company	

Can You Apply the Rule?

In each of the following groups, which name will be filed first and why?

1. San Francisco-Oakland Bay Bridge Authority
   San Francisco Opera Company

2. Virginia Beach Amusement Park   Virginia-Alexandria Realty

3. Lake Side Towing Service   Lake Superior Tours

Turn to page 47 to check your answers.

RULE 18. ADDRESSES

When two names are identical, alphabetize by comparing parts of addresses in the following order:

First: city or town

Second: state (Consider the state only if the city or town names are the same; for example, *Charleston, South Carolina,* and *Charleston, West Virginia.*)

Third: street name (If the street name is a number, treat it as if it were spelled out.)

Fourth: direction (For example, *north, south, northwest, southwest.*)

Fifth: house or building number (Arrange in numeric order from lowest to highest.)

NAME	UNIT 1	UNIT 2	UNIT 3	UNIT 4	UNIT 5	UNIT 6
Safeway Portland, Maine	Safeway	Portland	Maine			
Safeway Portland, Oregon	Safeway	Portland	Oregon			
Safeway 2083 Central Avenue Topeka, Kansas	Safeway	Topeka	Kansas	Central	Avenue	2083
Safeway 2100 Maryland Avenue Topeka, Kansas	Safeway	Topeka	Kansas	Maryland	Avenue	2100
Safeway 3267 Maryland Avenue Topeka, Kansas	Safeway	Topeka	Kansas	Maryland	Avenue	3267

Can You Apply the Rule?

In each of the following groups, which name will be filed first and why?

1. Rose's Dept. Store, Springfield, Massachusetts
   Rose's Dept. Store, Springfield, Missouri
2. James Palmer, 55 Michael Street, Oklahoma City, Oklahoma
   James Palmer, 1386 Michael Street, Tulsa, Oklahoma
3. Helpful Accounting Service, 34 Sheridan Drive, NW, Dallas, Texas
   Helpful Accounting Service, 48 Sheridan Drive, NE, Dallas, Texas

Turn to page 47 to check your answers.

━━━━━━━━━━ **FILING PRACTICE** ━━━━━━━━━━

Complete Jobs 8 and 9 of the *Practice Materials*. If the *Practice Materials* are not available, complete Exercise 8 on page 194 and Exercise 9 on page 195 of the Appendix.

After you have completed Jobs or Exercises 8 and 9, complete Job or Exercise 10.

RULE 19. BANKS AND OTHER FINANCIAL INSTITUTIONS

Consider each part of the name of a bank or other financial institution in the same order as it is written.

NAME	UNIT 1	UNIT 2	UNIT 3	UNIT 4
First National Bank of Rosemont	First	National	Bank	Rosemont
Montana National Bank, Billings	Montana	National	Bank	Billings
National Mortgage Co.	National	Mortgage	Company	
San Diego Trust & Savings	San	Diego	Trust	Savings

Can You Apply the Rule?

In each of the following groups, which name will be filed first and why?

1. Bank of California, Los Angeles   California Bank, La Jolla
2. West Branch Citizens Bank   East Branch Citizens Bank
3. Home Mortgage Company, Topeka
   Home Mortgage Company, Tallahassee

Turn to page 47 to check your answers.

RULE 20. HOTELS AND MOTELS

Consider each part of the name of a hotel or a motel in the same order as it is written. If the word *Hotel* or *Motel* appears at the beginning of the name, consider the distinctive part of the name first.

NAME	UNIT 1	UNIT 2	UNIT 3	UNIT 4
Hotel Paradise	Paradise	Hotel		
Royal Inn at the Wharf	Royal	Inn	Wharf	
Motel 7 of the Atlantic	Seven	Atlantic	Motel	
Surf and Sea Motel	Surf	Sea	Motel	
Tropical Island Paradise Hotel	Tropical	Island	Paradise	Hotel

Can You Apply the Rule?

In each of the following groups, which name will be filed first and why?

1. Hotel Sea Breeze   Sea Breeze Hotel
2. Hitching Post Hotel   Hitching Post Motel
3. Seven-Plus-One Motel   7th Avenue Motel

Turn to pages 47 and 48 to check your answers.

RULE 21. HOSPITALS AND RELIGIOUS INSTITUTIONS

Consider each part of the name of a hospital or a religious institution in the same order as it is written.

NAME	UNIT 1	UNIT 2	UNIT 3
Congregation Beth El	Congregation	Beth	El
Holy Cross Church	Holy	Cross	Church
Memorial Community Hospital	Memorial	Community	Hospital
Mercy Hospital and Home	Mercy	Hospital	Home
St. John's Hospital	Saint	John's	Hospital

Can You Apply the Rule?

In each of the following groups, which name will be filed first and why?

1. First Baptist Church of St. Louis   First Baptist Church
2. Medical Center Hospital   Center Medical Hospital
3. St. Mary's Church   St. Mary's Hospital

Turn to page 48 to check your answers.

RULE 22. EDUCATIONAL INSTITUTIONS

Consider each part of the name of a university, college, high school, elementary school, or library in the same order as it is written. If a word like *University* or *College* appears at the beginning of the name, consider the distinctive parts of the name first.

Note: Transpose names of individuals. (See Rule 3.)

NAME	UNIT 1	UNIT 2	UNIT 3	UNIT 4
Arizona State University	Arizona	State	University	
University of Arizona	Arizona	University		
MacDowell Elementary School	MacDowell	Elementary	School	
Jane Murphy Memorial Library	Murphy	Jane	Memorial	Library
School for the Visually Handicapped	Visually	Handicapped	School	

Can You Apply the Rule?

In each of the following groups, which name will be filed first and why?

1. Jack & Jill School   Jill Jackson Elementary School
2. University High School   University of San Diego
3. Library of Skyline Hills   Skyline Memorial Library

Turn to page 48 to check your answers.

 **FILING PRACTICE**

Complete Job 11 of the *Practice Materials*. If the *Practice Materials* are not available, complete Exercise 11 on page 195 of the Appendix.

RULE 23. FEDERAL GOVERNMENT NAMES

Index a name that pertains to the federal government under *United States Government* for the first three units. Then consider the name of the department, and finally the name of the bureau, division, commission, board, or other subdivision. In the following examples Unit 1 is *United,* Unit 2 is *States,* and Unit 3 is *Government.*

NAME	UNIT 4	UNIT 5	UNIT 6	UNIT 7
Civil Service Commission	Civil	Service	Commission	
Department of Labor, Bureau of Training	Labor	Department	Training	Bureau
Department of Transportation, Coast Guard	Transportation	Department	Coast	Guard

Can You Apply the Rule?

In each of the following groups, which name will be filed first? Why?

1. U.S. Government, Department of the Interior, National Park Service
   U.S. Government, Department of Agriculture, Food and Nutrition Service
2. U.S. Health and Human Resources Department, Food and Drug Administration
   U.S. Health and Human Resources Department, Social Security Administration
3. U.S. Treasury Department, Customs Service
   United States Steel Corporation

Turn to page 48 to check your answers.

RULE 24. STATE AND LOCAL GOVERNMENT NAMES

Index a name that pertains to a state, county, city, or town under the distinctive name, followed by the word *state, county, city, town,* or other classification. Consider the classification as an indexing unit whether or not it appears in the name as written. Finally, consider the name of the department, bureau, division, board, or other subdivision.

NAME	UNIT 1	UNIT 2	UNIT 3	UNIT 4	UNIT 5
State of New York, Board of Regents	New	York	State	Regents	Board
Parks Department, Ontario County	Ontario	County	Parks	Department	
Fire Department, Tampa	Tampa	City	Fire	Department	
State Education Dept., Tennessee	Tennessee	State	Education	Department	

Can You Apply the Rule?

In each of the following groups, which name will be filed first and why?

1. State of Nebraska, Transportation Dept.
   State of Nevada, Training Dept.
2. Bureau of Weights and Measures, Rockville County
   Sheriff's Dept., St. James County
3. Licenses and Permits, Town of Bloomington
   Chamber of Commerce, Bloomington

Turn to page 48 to check your answers.

RULE 25. FOREIGN GOVERNMENT NAMES

Consider a name that pertains to a foreign government first under the distinctive name of the country, followed by the classification *Dominion, Republic, Kingdom,* or other designation, then under the name of the governmental department or other subdivision.

Note: Not all foreign government names are followed by a designation, but most of them are. This designation would appear on the letterhead or be indicated in some other way on papers to be filed.

NAME	UNIT 1	UNIT 2	UNIT 3	UNIT 4
Dominion of Canada, Dept. of Education	Canada	Dominion	Education	Department
Republic of France, Dept. of State	France	Republic	State	Department

Can You Apply the Rule?

In each of the following groups, which name will be filed first and why?

1. Commonwealth of Australia, Ministry of Finance
   Australia Imports
2. Department of Industry and Commerce, Federal Republic of Brazil
   Department of Fisheries, Kingdom of Denmark
3. Department of Education, Federal Republic of Germany
   Ministry of Education, East German Democratic Republic

Turn to page 48 to check your answers.

━━━━━━━━━━ FILING PRACTICE ━━━━━━━━━━

Complete Job 12 of the *Practice Materials*. If the *Practice Materials* are not available, complete Exercise 12 on page 196 of the Appendix.

CROSS-REFERENCING BUSINESS AND SPECIAL NAMES

As with individual names, a record should be filed under the caption by which it is most likely to be requested. Cross-referencing business and special names may be necessary under the following circumstances:

1. When an organization is known by initials or other abbreviated name, it should be filed under the complete name and cross-referenced under the initials.

FILED UNDER	CROSS-REFERENCE
Young Men's Christian Association	YMCA

2. When the business may have some records under the name of an individual with the designation d/b/a (doing business as) while other records are filed according to the name of the business.

FILED UNDER	CROSS-REFERENCE
Jones' Auto Repair	Jones, John, d/b/a Jones' Auto Repair

3. When the name of the business or organization contains the complete name or initials of an individual and the name has been commonly used as the name of the business as it is written.

FILED UNDER	CROSS-REFERENCE
J. C. Penney	Penney, J. C., Company

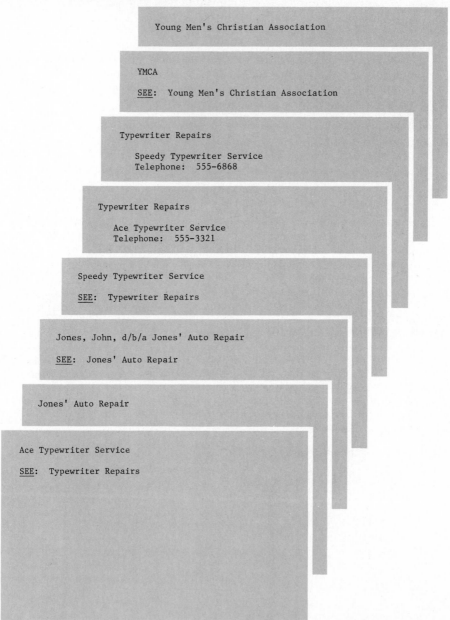

4. While records are usually considered to be filed under the name of
a business or individual, a subject heading may be more appropriate.
For example, an office may have one or more sources of typewriter
repairs, and keeping the information filed under a subject heading
would be more logical than dividing it among the companies that
actually do the work.

FILED UNDER	CROSS-REFERENCE
Typewriter Repairs	Ace Typewriter Service
Typewriter Repairs	Speedy Typewriter Service

5. When the business is known by a "coined" name or a name which differs from the dictionary spelling, the business would be filed according to the spelling it uses and cross-referenced under the dictionary spelling.

FILED UNDER	CROSS-REFERENCE
Bill's U-Rent	Bill's You-Rent
Bilt-In Furniture Shop	Built-In Furniture Shop
Cap'n Dooley Surf'n Shop	Captain Dooley Surfing Shop

6. When a business has a name change because of sale, incorporation, or other reason, you may need to cross-reference it under the old name until all records have been changed to the new name.

FILED UNDER	CROSS-REFERENCE
Quality Mart	(formerly) Crenshaw Meat Market
Sullivan and Mann Lumber Co.	(formerly) Sullivan, Robert, Wood Products

Can You Apply the Rule?

Indicate the file and cross-reference captions for each of the following names:

1. AAA (American Automobile Association)
2. Foliage and Flowers (formerly The Blossom Shop)
3. Geneva Phillips d/b/a Geneva's Country Inn
4. Office Supplies obtained from Printing and Stationery Company and Office Design and Equipment
5. R U Hungry Delicatessen
6. George Washington University

Turn to page 49 to check your answers.

FILING PRACTICE

Complete Job 13 of the *Practice Materials*. If the *Practice Materials* are not available, complete Exercise 13 on page 196 of the Appendix.
After you have completed Job or Exercise 13, complete Jobs or Exercises 14 to 16.

While the twenty-five rules you have just learned are used by most businesses and organizations in the United States, it is sometimes necessary to make modifications to meet particular needs. If many of your correspondents have similar names, you might file them according to a plan that would distribute them more evenly throughout the files. For example, banks having similar names could be filed first by the city and then by the name of the bank. Whatever variations are developed, it is important that they be followed consistently by everyone who uses your files.

ALPHABETIZING IN TELEPHONE DIRECTORIES

The basic rules for indexing are generally followed by telephone companies in compiling their directories. However, certain exceptions to the twenty-five indexing rules presented in Chapters 2 and 3 are observed for most directory listings. The most important exceptions are presented here so that you can locate telephone numbers quickly.

1. To meet common reference habits, at the customer's request, a complete individual name that is the first part of a firm name may be listed under the first name rather than the surname.

   Gordon Hall Associates (may be listed under *G*)
   John Marshall Hotel (may be listed under *J*)

2. Names that are spelled either as one or as two words are treated as spelled by the customer.

   Aero Space Supply precedes *Aerospace Fluids*.

3. Hyphenated words are split into separate units at the hyphen.

   Bel-Meade Apartments precedes *Beland, Roger*.

4. Single letters other than abbreviations are considered as separate indexing units. Single letters at the beginning of a firm name are treated independently of the rest of the name whether or not there are spaces between the letters, and the "nothing comes before something" rule applies for such groups.

   AA Vending Company precedes *AAA Dictation Systems*.

5. Organizations with numbers in their titles, such as unions, lodges, and clubs, are arranged alphabetically and are listed as shown in the following example:

   Carpenters Local Group Insurance precedes
   Carpenters Local 1358 which precedes
   Carpenters Local 1490.

6. The articles *a, an,* and *the* are considered units and are listed in the order in which they are written unless the customer requests oth-

erwise. For example, when *The* is the first word of a firm name, it may be dropped, placed at the end of the firm name, or, at the customer's request, left at the beginning of the name. It could even be listed in more than one place, if the customer requested this arrangement.

A World of Parts (listed under *A*)
The Supply Room (listed under *Supply Room, The* and *The Supply Room*)

7. Prepositions such as *by, for,* and *of* are considered units. Conjunctions such as *as,* and *or* (not *and*) are considered units. The conjunction *and,* often written *&,* is not considered in indexing.

Bank of Powatan precedes
Bank of the James, which precedes
Bank & Office Equipment.

PURPOSE OF FILING RULES

Now that you have completed your study of the twenty-five rules used for indexing individual, business, and special names, have you thought about the purpose of these rules? Try to visualize what would happen in an office if each person put records away using different rules or no rules at all. Records would become lost, many permanently; this, in turn, would cause disruptions in the office routine because of the time spent trying to locate files.

By giving you a pattern to follow, the rules assure that you will be able to file a name the same way every time. When you need to add a new name, you will be able to refer to the rules to guide you rather than having to guess where the records should be filed. Thus you will be able to keep records filed in an orderly and consistent pattern which will save time and money for your employer and will make you a more productive employee.

SURVEY OF COMPETENCIES

GENERAL REVIEW

You have had an opportunity to put into practice much of the material you have learned in this chapter. There are a few points, however, that you need to review to reinforce your learning of these concepts.

1. Name six instances when the cross-referencing of business and special names may be necessary.   (Competency 3)
2. Name three examples of the differences between the general indexing rules presented in this chapter and the listing of names in the telephone directory.   (Competency 4)
3. Why are indexing rules necessary? Have you ever lost a record because you did not file it properly?   (Competency 5)

You practiced Competencies 1 and 2 in the *Practice Materials* or Appendix exercises. The following indexing review will reinforce your ability to identify indexing units.

INDEXING REVIEW

A. What is the *first* indexing unit of each of the following names?

1. State Department, Washington, D.C.
2. Sun Shine Shade Co.
3. Mrs. Greer's Modeling School
4. The Tire Shop, Ltd.
5. 1-Way Car Rental
6. Blue Sea Motel
7. 55th Street Apartments
8. First National Bank of Atlantic City
9. K & B Equipment Company
10. University of Alaska

B. What is the *second* indexing unit of each of the following names?

1. Casa Del Mar Apartments
2. Chester, Dunn, and Lewis, Attorneys
3. Department of Education, Illinois
4. Dominion of Canada, Finance Department
5. United Methodist Church, Great Falls
6. Club 86
7. Jose Lopez Elementary School
8. Rath-Vermilyea Advertising Agency
9. North East Shopping Mall
10. Home Loan Credit Co.

C. What is the *third* indexing unit of each of the following names?

1. Grand Island Trailer Park
2. We-Guard-Your-Life Security Service
3. Eddie's Upholstery of St. Louis
4. University of North Carolina
5. KXTV Television Station
6. Cayuga County Board of Supervisors
7. Dr. Susan Wells' Clinic
8. 1900 Nostalgia Boutique
9. Hotel Sun and Sand
10. Rid a Bug Exterminators

D. Alphabetize the names in each of the following groups. On a separate sheet of paper, list the letters to indicate the correct alphabetic order.

1. a. Diamond's Department Store
   b. Diamonds-R-Forever Jewelry Store
   c. Jack of Diamonds Card Shop
2. a. Triangle Steel & Supply
   b. Tri-City Shopping Center
   c. Tricycle and Toy Shop
3. a. KNOR Radio Station
   b. KTAZ Television Station
   c. K-9 Dog Obedience School

4. a. St. John's Hospital, *2* Phoenix
   b. St. John's High School, *1* Philadelphia
   c. Mayor's Office, St. *3* Johnsbury, Vermont
5. a. Canadian Imports *2*
   b. Dominion of Canada, *1* Department of Trade
   c. Domestic Imports, Inc. *3*
6. a. Interstate Commerce *3* Commission, Washington, D.C. *v S 6*
   b. Inter State Trucking Co. *2*
   c. Inter-State Movers *1*
7. a. First National Bank, *2* Fargo, North Dakota *3*
   b. First Avenue Bank, *1* Fairmont, Texas
   c. First National Bank, Fairmont, Texas *2*

8. a. Dawn's Donut Shop, *3* 13 Third Avenue, Garden Grove, Kansas
   b. Dawn's Donut Shop, *1* 98 Third Avenue, Garden City, New York
   c. Dawn's Donut Shop, 1136 Third Avenue, *2* Garden City, New York
9. a. Hotel Jamestown (North *2* Dakota)
   b. Jamestown Hotel (New *1* York)
   c. Jamestown Inn *3*
10. a. Carson City High School *2*
    b. Carson City Police *3* Department
    c. Andrew Carson Art *1* Supplies

CASE PROBLEMS

1. You work for an insurance agency that writes policies for small local businesses. Your clients are primarily small firms that cater to a resort crowd and have unique names such as U R #1 (a fast-food hot dog stand), Mama Mia Whatta Resta Rant, and A Reel World (fishing equipment store). You have trouble finding some of these files. What helps could you devise to make these unusual names easier to locate? (Competencies 1, 2, 3, 4, 5)

2. You have a co-worker, Randy, who decides to file many pieces of correspondence his own way rather than following the rules you have learned. As a result, several important papers have been lost. How can you convince Randy to follow the rules? What will you do if you find that Randy never learned the filing rules? (Competencies 3, 5)

If you have not mastered all of the competencies reviewed in the Survey, reread that part of the chapter which deals with the competency in question; then recheck your progress.

ANSWERS TO CAN YOU APPLY THE RULE?

RULE 9

1. Raymond **Bigelow** Imports, **Mr.** Big Restaurant; *Bigelow* comes before *Mr.* since you transpose the parts of a complete name.
2. **Mrs.** Plants Flowers, **Plant** House Flowers; *Mrs.* comes before *Plants* since you consider a title in a firm name as an indexing unit.

3. University **Auto** Leasing, University **Automobile** Leasing; nothing comes before something.

RULE 10

1. El Patio Restaurant, **P**atio and Restaurant Shop; *El* is an indexing unit.
2. Pet **Shop**, A Pet **Shoppe**; the article *A* is disregarded.
3. The Leisure Reading Store, **Th**y Leisure Reading Store; the article *The* is disregarded, but the noncontemporary word *Thy* is a unit.

RULE 11

1. Data Systems **Manufacturers**, Data Systems **Manufacturing** Division; *Mfg.* spelled out follows *Manufacturers*.
2. Walker Company, Incorporated; Walker, **O.** M., Company, Incorporated; the second units are different.
3. Brother Martin Company, **Martin** Brothers Company; a title is the first indexing unit if it is used with only one part of an individual's name. (See Rule 6.)

RULE 12

1. ABC **D**iaper Service, A B C **T**oy Store; since the first three units are identical, the fourth units determine the filing order.
2. **A** to Z Research Service, **E**verything A to Z; the first units determine the order.
3. B J Gifts, **Blue** Jay Florist and Gifts; nothing comes before something.

RULE 13

1. **R**obert-Wade Jewelry Story, Robert **W**ade Hardware Store; the name of an individual must be transposed for filing; the hyphenated name is one unit.
2. **Do** It Yourself Hobby Store, **Do-I**t-Yourself Shop; without the hyphens, *Do It Yourself* is three units and with the hyphens it is one unit.
3. **Manuel**-Ramirez Co., **M-R** Company; each name has only two units because of the hyphens, and you need to consider the units letter by letter.

RULE 14

1. Seacoast **G**ift Shop, Sea Coast **R**estaurant; even though it is written as two words, *Sea Coast* is one unit and the second units determine the filing sequence.
2. **Sky** Pike Trucking Company, **Sky Line** Boating Company; *Sky* and *Pike* are two separate units (they could be hyphenated, but they do not make sense as one word), and *Sky Line* is one unit.
3. Inter Lake Steam Ship Company, Interlake Steamship **Manufactur**ers; third units need to be considered.

RULE 15

1. **I.** T.'s Hair Fashions, **It's** About Time Watch Repair; nothing comes before something.

2. Hasting's Appliance **Service**, Hastings' Appliance **St**ore; the third units determine the filing order.
3. Bob Davids' **P**hoto Mart, David's **P**hoto Mart; the second units are different.

RULE 16

1. **Four** Seasons Nursery, **Fourth** Avenue Garage; the numbers are considered as spelled out.
2. **Seven** Rider Carpool Service, **Seven-Day** Repair Service; the hyphenated name determines the filing order.
3. Apartment House **Eighteen** hundred eighty-three, Apartment House **Eighty**-three; the numbers are filed as they are spelled out, not from lowest to highest.

RULE 17

1. **San Francisco** Opera Company, **San Francisco-O**akland Bay Bridge Authority; the hyphen creates a "nothing comes before something" situation with the second units.
2. **Virginia** Beach Amusement Park, **Virginia-A**lexandria Realty; *Virginia Beach* is two units while *Virginia-Alexandria* is one unit.
3. **Lake** Superior Tours, **Lake Side** Towing Service; in this case *Lake Side* is one unit because it can be spelled as one word. (See Rule 14.)

RULE 18

1. Rose's Department Store, Springfield, **Ma**ssachusetts; Rose's Department Store, Springfield, **Mi**ssouri; the state determines the filing order.
2. James Palmer, 55 Michael Street, **O**klahoma City, Oklahoma; James Palmer, 1386 Michael Street, **T**ulsa, Oklahoma; the city is the determining unit.
3. Helpful Accounting Service, 48 Sheridan Drive, **Northe**ast, Dallas, Texas; Helpful Accounting Service, 34 Sheridan Drive, **Northw**est, Dallas, Texas; the direction determines the filing order before the street number is used.

RULE 19

1. **B**ank of California, Los Angeles; **C**alifornia Bank, La Jolla; the first units are different even though the names are similar.
2. **E**ast Branch Citizens Bank, **W**est Branch Citizens Bank; the first units are different.
3. Home Mortgage Company, **Ta**llahassee; Home Mortgage Company, **To**peka; the cities are the determining indexing units.

RULE 20

1. Sea Breeze Hotel or Sea Breeze, Hotel; in this case the names for filing purposes are identical and it would be necessary to check the address for a determining unit.
2. Hitching Post **H**otel, Hitching Post **M**otel; if two names are identical except for the words *Hotel* and *Motel,* then the logical order is *Hotel* before *Motel.*

3. **Seven-Plus-One** Motel, **Seventh** Avenue Motel; the number needs to be spelled out to determine the filing order.

RULE 21
1. **First Baptist Church, First Baptist Church** of Saint Louis; nothing comes before something.
2. Center Medical Hospital, Medical Center Hospital; the first units are sufficient for determining the filing order.
3. Saint Mary's Church, Saint Mary's Hospital; in this case, the third unit determines the filing sequence.

RULE 22
1. **Jack** & Jill School, Jill **Jacks**on Elementary School; the "nothing comes before something" rule applies to first units.
2. San Diego, University (of), **University** High School; in this case University is a distinctive part of the name of the high school and therefore an indexing unit.
3. Skyline Hills, Library (of); Skyline **Memorial** Library; the distinctive parts of the name are considered first, and so the second units determine the order.

RULE 23
1. **Agriculture** comes before **Interior**.
2. U.S. Government, Health and Human Resources Administration is the same in both names, and **Food** comes before **Social**.
3. United States **Government** comes before United States **Steel** Corporation; not all names which have *United States* or *U.S.* in the name are part of the federal government.

RULE 24
1. **Nebr**aska, State, Transportation Department; **Nev**ada, State, Training Department; the states are the only units which need to be considered in this case.
2. **Rockville**, County, Weights (and) Measures, Bureau (of); **Saint** James County, Sheriff's Department; the names of the counties determine the filing order.
3. Bloomington, Town (of), Licenses (and) Permits; **Chamber** (of) Commerce, Bloomington; *Chamber of Commerce* is a private organization.

RULE 25
1. Australia, **Commonwealth** (of), Finance, Ministry (of); Australia **Im**ports; the classification of the country is the second indexing unit in the first name which determines the indexing order. *Australia Imports* is a private organization.
2. **Brazil**, Federal Republic (of), Industry (and) Commerce, Department (of); **Denmark**, Kingdom (of), Fisheries, Department (of); *Brazil* comes before *Denmark*.
3. **East** German Democratic Republic; **Germany**, Federal Republic (of); the distinctive name of the country is the first indexing unit.

CROSS-REFERENCING BUSINESS AND SPECIAL NAMES

FILED UNDER	CROSS-REFERENCE
1. American Automobile Association	AAA
2. Foliage and Flowers	Blossom Shop (The)
3. Geneva's Country Inn	Phillips, Geneva, d/b/a Geneva's Country Inn
4. Office Supplies	Office Design and Equipment
Office Supplies	Printing and Stationery Company
5. R U Hungry Delicatessen	Are You Hungry Delicatessen
6. George Washington University	Washington, George, University

4

Managing Correspondence

COMPETENCIES

When you have completed this chapter, you will be able to:

1. State the differences among incoming, outgoing, and internal correspondence.
2. Give examples of how businesses organize records according to alphabetic, numeric, subject, and geographic filing.
3. Describe how to set up file drawers and list the equipment necessary. Prepare file folder labels. (See Job 17 of the *Practice Materials*.)
4. List and describe the steps in the path of an incoming letter.
5. List and describe the steps in the filing process.
6. List and describe the steps for storing correspondence in an alphabetic filing system.
7. Index and code correspondence for filing, prepare cross-references, and practice filing and finding correspondence. (See Jobs 18 to 22 of the *Practice Materials*.)

CLASSIFYING CORRESPONDENCE

Correspondence may be classified according to whether it is incoming, outgoing, or for internal distribution.

Incoming correspondence includes such items as letters, mailgrams, contracts, reports, or employment applications. Catalogs, price lists, brochures, newspapers, and magazines and other third-class mail pieces are also incoming correspondence, though most of these items are kept temporarily and discarded without filing.

Outgoing correspondence includes the same items as incoming except of course that they are sent rather than received.

Mail for internal distribution will include many memos, in addition to other business papers.

ORGANIZING RECORDS FOR STORING

In Chapter 1 you learned that the four main filing systems are alphabetic, subject, numeric, and geographic. These systems define the basic ways in which records are organized and stored for efficient retrieval of needed information. Thus in a school system where data on students was needed, an alphabetic system with students' names as folder captions would be selected. A purchasing agent responsible for buying hundreds of products would select a subject system with product names for folder captions. A real estate agent would select a geographic system with cities or districts or street names as captions, depending upon the area served. And an insurance company would select a numeric system, since insurance policies are identified by number. In all these examples, records are organized so that they are easy to find when needed.

Whatever the needs of business or the organization, records are filed according to the rules for indexing individual, business, and special names you studied in Chapters 2 and 3.

SETTING UP FILE DRAWERS

Most paper records are housed in file cabinets or on open shelves. Nonpaper records such as magnetic tape reels or microfilm are housed in specially designed equipment. Whatever the type of equipment used, however, the main purpose is to make it easy to retrieve information when it is needed. In this chapter you will consider the basic arrangement of paper records stored in a file drawer. Basic equipment necessary for setting up a file drawer consists of file drawer labels, guides, folders, and folder labels.

FILE DRAWER LABELS. Each drawer should be properly labeled so that the contents can be identified quickly. The caption on the label indicates the alphabetic range of the records housed there. Suppose the drawer contains records that begin with the name *Dabney* and end with the name *Furman*. The label or caption can be written either (1) as a single caption, with the single letter *D* to indicate where in the alphabet the records begin, or (2) as a double, or closed caption, with the two letters *D* and *F,* usually hyphenated *D-F* to indicate where the sequence begins and ends.

FILE DRAWER GUIDES. In correspondence files, cardboard or pressboard sheets called *guides* serve two purposes:

1. They separate the file drawer into distinct labeled sections which make it easier to locate specific records.
2. They support the records to prevent them from bowing and sagging.

Guide Tabs, Cuts, and Positions. Extending above the top edge of a correspondence guide is a *tab,* which identifies the alphabetic range of the records to be stored behind it. The guides are somewhat larger than the file folder and are described by the width of the tab, commonly called the *cut.* A *one-fifth cut* means that the tab extends along one-fifth of the top edge of the guide. A *one-third cut* means that the tab occupies one-third of the guide's top edge, and so on. A tab occupying the first one-fifth of the left edge of the guide as you face the file is said to be in *first position;* the second tab in the second one-fifth position from the left is said to be in *second position;* the third tab from the left, in *third position,* and so on. Guides are said to be in a staggered arrangement when their tabs are in successive positions reading from left to right, as shown in the illustrations at the bottom of this page.

Guide Captions. Guide captions which are written or printed on the guide tabs identify the records filed behind them. In some systems the caption can be typed or printed on a small strip of paper, then placed into a metal or plastic holder on the guide.

TAB CUTS AND POSITIONS OF GUIDES

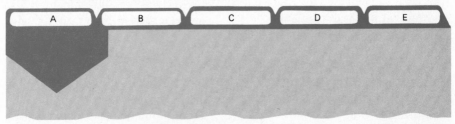

One-fifth cut staggered guides with single captions. Starting at the left, guides are in first, second, third, fourth, and fifth positions.

One-third cut staggered guides with double captions. Starting at the left, guides are in first, second, and third positions.

On guides, the captions may be either single or double as they are on the file drawer. Captions may be words as well as letters. They should, however, be kept short for quick, easy reading. Single captions indicate where each section begins. The records to be filed after a single caption are those beginning with the caption on the guide tab up to, but not including, the caption on the next guide tab. The use of single guide captions makes expansion of the file easy because additional guides can be inserted wherever another subdivision is needed. Single captions may be easier to read than double captions because they can be larger and thus more legible on the tabs. The advantage of the double caption is that it allows you to see the entire range of the section covered by a guide without looking at the next guide.

FILE FOLDERS.   File folders serve as containers for correspondence in the files. They are made of heavy paper that is folded so that all or part of the top edge of the back extends ½ inch or more above the front to form a tab. At the bottom of the folder are several horizontal creases called *scores* that permit expansion of the folder to hold up to 100 sheets of correspondence. The correct way to break the first score on a folder is shown in the illustration below. After about 50 sheets of paper have been placed in the folder, the second score should be broken to accommodate the additional 50 sheets in the folder.

Folder Tabs.   The projecting tab on the back of the folder provides a place for the title, or caption, of the folder contents. This caption is usually typed on a folder label, and the label is attached to the tab. Folders, like file guides, are available with tabs of various widths, or cuts. Folders can also be obtained with tabs in any one of the several positions along the top edge

BREAKING THE FIRST SCORE ON A FILE FOLDER

(1) Papers curl if scores on a file folder are broken too soon. (2) Papers ride up if scores are not broken soon enough. (3) When about twenty-five papers are filed, break the first score, and papers will stand straight.

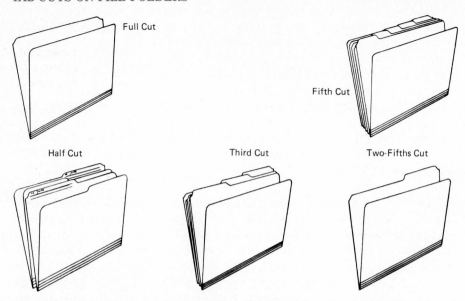

of the folder. Files may be arranged so that the tabs are in a staggered arrangement, or they may be arranged so that the tabs are all in the same position. Different types of folder tabs are shown in the illustration above.

Folder Labels. Gummed labels for folder captions, usually about 4 inches wide, are available in perforated strips, adhesive strips, or continuous rolls. Each kind of label is available in a variety of colors or in white with colored borders. High-speed data-processing equipment can print captions on long strips of file labels. If you do not have ready-made labels, you will find the suggestions below and on page 55 helpful in the preparation of file folder labels. You may at some time use labels which are folded into a front and back portion. The wider portion, if there is a difference, is always the front of the label and is the one on which the caption is typed.

Here are some suggestions for typing folder labels:

1. Start typing the caption on the third space from the left edge of the label and on the second line below the top edge or crease. The caption should be started at the same place on every tab. Some tabs, particularly those that are white with a colored border, have small white marks in the border to indicate typing alignment. You may use these to achieve consistent placement of information on the label. Thus all first words on tabs of the same position will be in a straight line when they are placed in a file drawer. This makes it easier to read the labels and to locate the file you need and also creates a neater and more uniform appearance. The illustration at the top of page 55 shows correctly typed labels.
2. The words of the items in the caption are typed in indexing order.

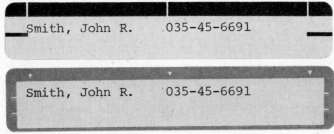

Smith, John R.   035-45-6691

Smith, John R.   035-45-6691

Notice how they are typed to follow the markings on the label.

3. In some offices, the entire first line of a label is capitalized; in others, only the first letter of each important word. The style selected should be used consistently.

4. In some offices, punctuation, including the period after abbreviations, is omitted entirely, with two spaces left where the punctuation would have been. Most offices use normal punctuation. Again, follow the style used by your office.

5. Block style is preferred if the caption includes more than one item. If any item in the caption runs over to a second line, these words

FOLDER CAPTIONS CORRECTLY TYPED AND ALIGNED

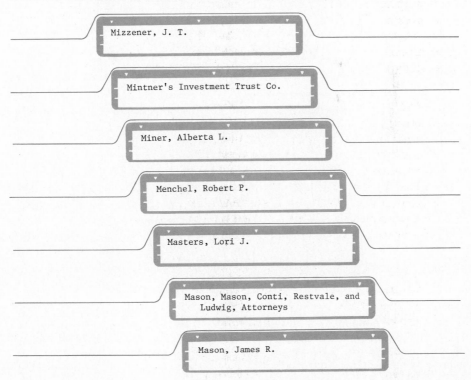

Mizzener, J. T.

Mintner's Investment Trust Co.

Miner, Alberta L.

Menchel, Robert P.

Masters, Lori J.

Mason, Mason, Conti, Restvale, and
Ludwig, Attorneys

Mason, James R.

should be indented three spaces for clarity. Correctly typed and aligned folder captions are shown in the illustration on page 55.

You are now ready to complete Job 17 of the *Practice Materials*.

ORGANIZING GUIDES AND FOLDERS

Alphabetic correspondence files generally have these elements: (1) primary guides; (2) special guides, also known as secondary or auxiliary guides; (3) individual folders; and (4) miscellaneous folders. These parts are shown in the illustration below.

BASIC ALPHABETIC CORRESPONDENCE FILE DRAWER ARRANGEMENT

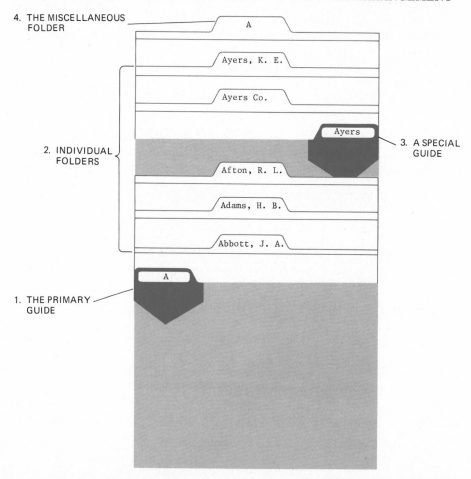

(1) The *primary guide* is located in front of the group of folders and special guides it controls. (2) *Individual folders* come *after* the guide and are arranged alphabetically. (3) A *special guide* is located in front of frequently consulted individual folders. (4) The *miscellaneous folder* comes *after* the individual folders. It has the same caption as the primary guide.

PRIMARY GUIDES. In order to divide the file drawer into major alphabetic sections, primary guides are placed at the beginning of each section. If a file is small, it might be divided into only twenty-six sections, the first being *A*. (In large filing systems, you may find several primary guides for each of the twenty-six alphabetic divisions. For example, the primary guides under the letter *A* could be *Aa, Ae, Ai, Ao, Au.*) The *A* primary guide tells the file worker that all records behind it, up to the primary guide *B,* concern those correspondents whose names begin with *A*. The tabs for primary guides are usually at the extreme left.

In general, each primary guide should have at least five but not more than ten folders behind it. Files become cumbersome and expensive to maintain where there are fewer than five folders behind each guide. When there are too many folders behind one guide, the advantages of rapid location and proper support of the folders are lost.

SPECIAL GUIDES. Special, auxiliary, or secondary guides are used after a primary guide to subdivide that section or to highlight names that are frequently referred to. A special or auxiliary guide may be placed in any of the "cut" positions, depending on the arrangement of the file and the purpose of the guide.

INDIVIDUAL FOLDERS. After each guide are the individual folders arranged alphabetically. An individual folder is not prepared until at least five records relating to a particular correspondent or subject have been received. In an alphabetic correspondence file, you will recognize the individual folders quickly because their tabs contain the full names of correspondents and because the tabs are usually wider than those on guides and miscellaneous folders. The position of the tabs on individual folders is ordinarily at the center or to the right of center. The records in individual folders are arranged chronologically with the latest date in front so that the most recent correspondence will be easy to locate.

MISCELLANEOUS FOLDERS. At the end of every group of individual folders, there is a miscellaneous folder. These folders are for the correspondents who fall within the area defined by the primary guide, but who do not have a sufficient number of records to warrant an individual folder. Miscellaneous folder tabs are usually to the left of the individual folder tabs. The records within miscellaneous folders are arranged alphabetically according to the name of the correspondent. If there is more than one record for a correspondent in the miscellaneous folder, these records are arranged chronologically with the most recent first as in an individual folder.

PATH OF A LETTER

What happens to a piece of correspondence when it is received by the office staff? First, the incoming mail is processed. Then the letter is used for business purposes. When the individual using the letter is finished, the letter is "released" for filing. The last step before the actual filing process

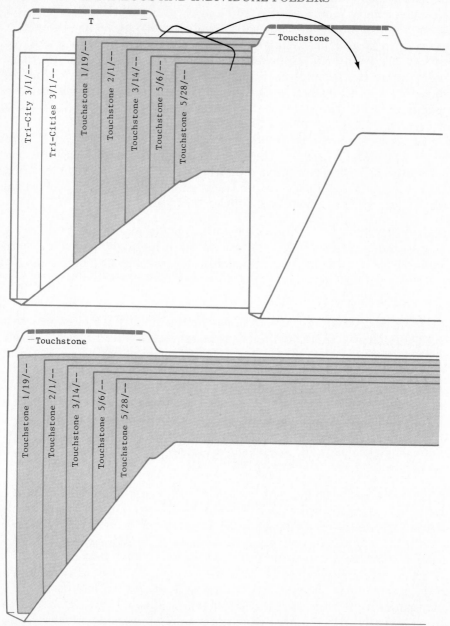

Since there are five letters from Touchstone Office Supplies in the Miscellaneous *T* folder, an individual folder is opened for that company and the letters are transferred to it. Letters in the individual folder are arranged by date, with the latest date in front.

is the collection of the correspondence to be filed. These steps are shown in the illustration on the next page.

Incoming correspondence is opened. The paper is then date-stamped and delivered to the user.

The user attends to the correspondence, places release marks on the paper to be filed, and places the paper in the out basket for delivery to the files.

PROCESSING INCOMING CORRESPONDENCE. Most organizations have a procedure for handling incoming correspondence. This procedure usually includes the following steps:

1. Correspondence received in a central mail department is sorted and distributed unopened to the various offices. Mail which is not identified is opened and then routed to the proper location.
2. Within each office, the secretary or another individual will open and process the mail by:
   a. Checking to see that a return address is on the correspondence or the envelope.
   b. Dating and time stamping the correspondence to verify receipt.
   c. Checking for enclosures.
   d. Checking to see whether it can be handled by that office or needs to be routed to another office.

RELEASING CORRESPONDENCE FOR FILING. After the mail has been processed, it is used by someone to conduct the business of the organization. After the correspondence has been used, it is released for filing. A notation that the letter is ready to be filed is known as a *release mark*. A common release mark is the initials of the person using the record for the first time. These initials are placed in the upper left-hand corner of the letter. Other release marks can be used, but it is important that the same mark be used consistently. Release marks are not necessary on carbons or photocopies of outgoing letters and interoffice memorandums.

It is important to remember that not all items of incoming correspondence or carbon copies of outgoing correspondence need to be filed. Many routine acknowledgments and relatively unimportant communications are discarded after they have been read or answered. The decision of whether or not to file should be made by the executive who handles the correspondence. Detailed information about transfer and disposal of records will be discussed in Chapter 9, "Records Control and Retention."

COLLECTING CORRESPONDENCE FOR FILING. A special folder, out basket, or other means of designating material ready for filing should be used. A definite routine for collecting correspondence to be filed should be developed so that materials will be available in the files when needed. This policy is especially important in a large corporation where thousands of pieces of correspondence are handled every day and where the work of hundreds of people is affected by the availability of records.

STEPS IN THE FILING PROCESS

After correspondence has been released for filing, it travels through five distinct steps: (1) inspecting, (2) indexing, (3) coding, (4) sorting, and (5) storing. These steps are illustrated on page 61. All these steps will be followed by the individual who works with the files, whether a secretary in a small office or a filing specialist in a large company.

1. Inspecting.   Correspondence is checked to make sure it has been released for filing.

2. Indexing.   The name by which the correspondence will most likely be requested from the files is determined. In this example it was decided that *Touchstone Office Supplies, Incorporated* would be the caption under which the letter would be filed.

3. Coding.   The caption determined in the indexing step is underscored.

   The cross-reference caption is underscored, and an *X* is placed at the end of the line.

4. Sorting.   All correspondence to be filed is sorted in alphabetic order according to the underscored captions.

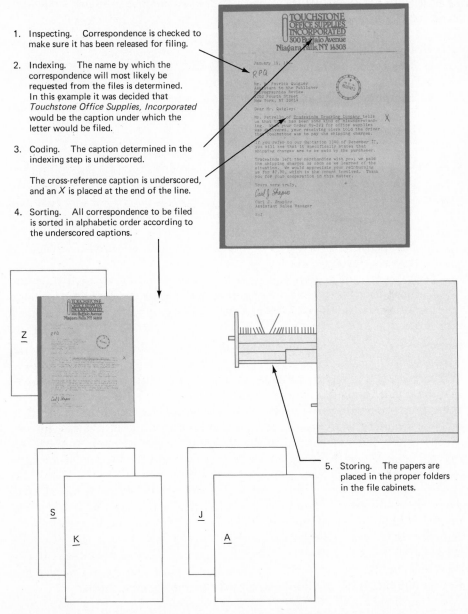

5. Storing.   The papers are placed in the proper folders in the file cabinets.

INSPECTING.   Each piece of correspondence must be checked for the release mark before being filed. If it has not been released, it should be returned to the person to whom it was assigned. The release mark is the authority to file.

INDEXING.   When you learned the twenty-five filing rules, you practiced indexing the names you filed in your practice jobs or exercises. Indexing, therefore, is the mental process by which you determine the name, subject, or other caption under which a piece of correspondence is to be filed.

There are several different clues to help you determine the caption:

1. The name on the letterhead (incoming correspondence)
2. The name of the person or organization addressed (outgoing)
3. The name in the signature (incoming)
4. The name of the subject discussed (incoming or outgoing)
5. The name of the geographic location about which the correspondence is concerned (incoming or outgoing)

CODING. Indexing is the mental process of determining the caption under which the correspondence is to be filed. Writing or otherwise indicating the caption on the correspondence is known as *coding*. There are two common methods of coding correspondence for alphabetic systems:

1. The caption, or name to be indexed, can be underlined, preferably with a colored pencil.
2. If the caption under which the correspondence should be filed is not mentioned in the body of the message or does not appear anywhere on the paper, the caption is written in the upper right-hand corner.

Cross-Referencing. Correspondence should always be indexed and coded by the caption under which it is most likely to be requested from the files. Whenever a paper may be called for in one or more different ways, it should be filed under the most frequently used caption and cross-referenced under the others. You will recall that cross-referencing means placing a sheet of paper containing information about the actual location of a document (or a copy of the document) in all places in a file where a person might want to look for it. When it is necessary to cross-reference the piece of correspondence, the caption under which it is actually placed in the file should be underlined or written as explained in 1 and 2 above. The caption selected for the cross-reference should also be underlined or written, and in addition, an *x* should be placed at the end of the line or after the written caption to indicate that it is a cross-reference. A cross-reference sheet or a copy of the correspondence should be prepared at the same time. Most offices use a form such as the cross-reference sheet shown in the illustration on page 63 so that complete information is recorded in a consistent manner.

SORTING. Sorting is the process of arranging the records in alphabetic order after they have been coded. This speeds up the process of placing correspondence in the files. Rough and fine sorting of cards was explained in Chapter 2. The procedure for sorting correspondence is the same. In offices where there is a large volume of correspondence to be readied for the files, special sorting devices and equipment are used to simplify and speed up sorting.

CROSS-REFERENCE SHEET

Name or Subject   Date
  Tradewinds Trucking Company   1/19/19--

Regarding
  Shipping charges on Order 89-223

SEE
Name or Subject
  Touchstone Office Supplies, Inc.
  300 Buffalo Avenue
  Niagara Falls, NY 14300

File cross-reference sheet under name or subject at top of the sheet and
by the latest date of papers. Describe matter for identification purposes.
The papers, themselves, should be filed under name or subject after "SEE."

Made in U.S.A.

STORING. The last step in the filing process, storing, is the actual placement of the records in the files. Correspondence is normally stored in file
folders. You should follow these step-by-step directions for storing records
in file folders:

1. Take the sorted records to the proper file drawer, cross-check the
   label with the sorted record, and open the file drawer.
2. Using the guide captions as locators, scan the folder tabs until the
   caption under which the correspondence is to be stored is located.
   Guides, even those with metal tabs, should be handled as much as
   possible from the sides so that the tabs do not become bent and
   smudged. Occasionally, you should straighten the contents of the
   file drawer by pulling the bottoms of small groups of folders forward
   until they stand upright in the drawer.
3. Raise the folder (do not pull the tab of the folder since this will
   cause it to break off eventually) and rest it on the edge of the drawer.

Managing Correspondence 63

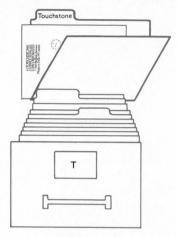

1. Locate the proper file drawer, using the guide captions as locators. Raise the desired folder and rest it on the drawer side.

2. Compare the caption on the record to be filed with the caption on the record in the folder.

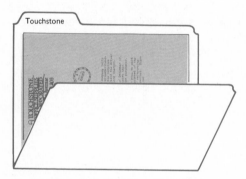

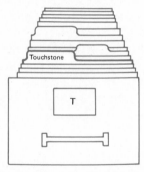

3. Place the record in the folder with the heading to the left.

4. Carefully slide the folder back to the original position. Close drawer.

4. Be sure that you have the proper folder. Compare the caption on the folder with the caption on the record being stored and with the caption on the top record already in the folder. Checking will take only a few seconds—time that may prevent many records from being misfiled and thus lost.

5. Place the record carefully in the folder with the heading to the left as you face the file so that the left side of the record will rest on the bottom of the folder. Within the individual folder, the most recent correspondence is placed on top; in other words, a letter dated October 23 would be placed on top of one dated October 15 of the same year. Placing the letterhead to the left of the folder assures that it will be in correct reading position when the folder is pulled from the file and opened. Remember, overcrowding a folder causes the contents to ride up and obscure the caption and makes the folder difficult to handle.

6. Replace the folder so that it rests on the bottom of the drawer with the sides in a vertical position and the caption fully visible. If there is no individual folder for the record, all the individual folders in the section are pulled forward, exposing the miscellaneous folder for the section. The record is then placed inside the miscellaneous folder. The miscellaneous folder is placed behind the individual folders so that time is not lost looking for it if there is no individual folder for that particular record. Within the miscellaneous folder, correspondence is filed alphabetically. If there are two or more pieces of correspondence for the same name, the most recent is placed on top as in the individual folder. When five pieces of correspondence for the same name accumulate, usually an individual folder is set up and the correspondence is removed from the miscellaneous folder and placed in the proper place in the file drawer.

Some file workers like to use the bookmark method of removing file folders. In this procedure, the folder is lifted but, instead of being removed completely, it is raised at one end until the end rests on the edge of the drawer with about one-third of the folder exposed. In this position the file worker can insert the piece of correspondence in the folder and return it to its proper location. The bookmark method has the advantage of maintaining the folder's proper position in the file, thereby saving time.

FILING PRACTICE

If you are using the *Practice Materials* which accompany this textbook, you are now ready to complete Jobs 18 to 22.

SURVEY OF COMPETENCIES

GENERAL REVIEW

The following questions will help you to reinforce your learning of the competencies included in this chapter.

1. What items are included in incoming correspondence? Outgoing correspondence? Internal correspondence? What distinguishes each from the other two types? (Competency 1)
2. What are the four basic ways in which records may be organized? Give an example of each of these uses in the business world. (Competency 2)
3. What is the main purpose of filing equipment? (Competency 3)
4. Give an example of a single caption and a double caption. (Competency 3)
5. What are the two purposes of file drawer guides? (Competency 3)

6. What is a *tab?* What is a *cut?* What does *first position* mean? (Competency 3)
7. What is the purpose of *guide captions?* (Competency 3)
8. What purpose do file folders serve? What are *scores?* What information is shown on a folder tab? (Competency 3)
9. How should you type information on file folder labels? (Competency 3)
10. What is the purpose of *primary guides?* What is the purpose of *special guides?* What is the purpose of *miscellaneous folders?* (Competency 3)
11. What are the steps for processing incoming correspondence? (Competency 4)
12. What is a *release mark?* Why is it important in the filing process? Are all items of correspondence filed? (Competency 4)
13. Why is a routine for collecting correspondence for filing necessary? (Competency 4)
14. List and describe the steps in the filing process. (Competency 5)
15. List five clues to help you determine the caption of a piece of correspondence. (Competency 5)
16. What are two common methods for coding correspondence? (Competency 5)
17. How do you cross-reference correspondence? (Competency 5)
18. List and describe the steps for storing correspondence. (Competency 6)
19. What is the minimum number of records for an individual folder? How are these records arranged within the folder? (Competency 6)
20. What is the *bookmark method?* (Competency 6)

CASE PROBLEMS

1. Your friend Marsha Persky has recently begun work in a small office. As she is having some problems with the filing system, she asks your advice one day. You try to pinpoint the problem. She gives you the following information:

   a. She can't read the labels on some folders because the correspondence in the folders rides up and covers them.
   b. Some folders are too low in the drawer and she has been missing them when filing. She then has to go back and look through the drawer again.
   c. She has to open two, sometimes three, drawers to find where a particular folder should be stored. The captions of the drawers are a single letter and there are three or four drawers labeled with the same letter.
   d. She needs to go through the entire drawer to find where a folder should be stored.
   e. When there is no folder for a piece of correspondence, she is to make a new one even if there is only one letter to put in the

folder. Miscellaneous folders are placed immediately after the primary guide for that section of the file drawer; these folders are empty for the most part.

f.   There seems to be no organization to the contents of the folders.

What advice and suggestions can you give Marsha? (Competencies 3, 6)

2.   Raymond DeVere works in the central filing department of a large company. Many people see correspondence before it is filed. His job is to sort the correspondence, code it, and make sure that it gets stored properly. There have been some problems lately about correspondence which was not replaced in the files after the individual responsible was finished with it and which was therefore not available when needed by others in the company. In addition, some items have been filed before action was taken. Raymond has been reprimanded for these situations, but since he files only what is brought to him by the various departments, he feels the criticism is unfair. What can he do, if anything, to help avoid these situations in the future? (Competencies 4, 5)

If you have not mastered all of the competencies reviewed in the Survey, reread that part of the chapter which deals with the competency in question; then recheck your progress.

5

Managing Card Records and Business Forms

When you have completed this chapter, you will be able to:

1. State what is meant by *card records* and list the advantages of card records; give examples of uses of card records.
2. Name and describe the categories and sizes of card records.
3. Compare and contrast vertical and visible files.
4. State what is meant by printed guide words and variable information on business forms.
5. State the purposes and uses of business forms and give examples of forms used in businesses.

CARD RECORDS

A person often thinks of correspondence in connection with filing and records management. However, much information is recorded and stored on cards. Card records and business forms are used for both internal and external purposes to tabulate, record, or transmit information as briefly and quickly as possible in a standardized, understandable format. This chapter will discuss the types and uses of card records and the characteristics and uses of business forms.

DEFINITION OF CARD RECORDS. Card records are distinguished from correspondence in two ways: (1) They are smaller in size, and a heavier weight of paper is used for them. (2) They are not kept in folders as is correspondence. Card files are used both as indexes to correspondence filing systems and as independent records.

ADVANTAGES OF CARD RECORDS. For organizing information, a card file has the following advantages:

1. Information can be inserted easily by the preparation of a new card.
2. Information can be deleted quickly by the destruction of an old card.
3. Information can be rearranged in any sequence—alphabetic, geographic, numeric, or subject.
4. A group of cards can be used by several workers simultaneously.
5. Some cards are designed so that they can be placed in certain business machines for automatic sorting, posting of data, and processing.

PURPOSES OF CARD RECORDS. Card records may be catagorized as *index card records* or *posted card records,* according to the purpose they serve.

Index Card Records. Cards that are used to provide reference information are called *index card records*. The information on them does not change frequently. Examples are the secretary's address file, the index to numeric correspondence files, and the card index in a library.

Posted Card Records. Cards on which information is continually recorded are called *posted card records*. They too provide reference information, but the information on posted card records frequently changes. Posted card records are usually consulted for up-to-date information.

Posted card records, which are illustrated at the bottom of page 71, are used in business whenever there is a large number of products, customers, facts and figures, or other items to be referred to. For example, many firms have card files in their purchasing departments. On the cards in these files are names of suppliers and purchases made from them.

Sales records also are kept on cards, and from them management can easily determine sales volume according to territory, product, department, or salesperson. The cards need only to be rearranged to produce various categories of information. Sometimes customer accounts are kept on cards that are placed in a machine for daily posting of both sales and receipts. A copy of the card may be sent to the customer at the end of the month as a bill. Inventory records are kept on cards so that records about new products can easily be added, records about discontinued products can be removed, and the quantity of a product on hand can be kept up to date on an independent record.

Payroll records are another example of posted card records. A separate card for each employee contains such information as the names and ages of dependents, current salary, job title, and date of employment.

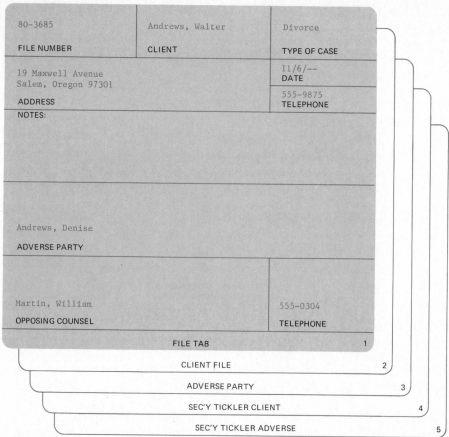

80-3685		Andrews, Walter		Divorce	
FILE NUMBER		CLIENT		TYPE OF CASE	

19 Maxwell Avenue	11/6/--
Salem, Oregon 97301	DATE
	555-9875
ADDRESS	TELEPHONE

NOTES:

Andrews, Denise
ADVERSE PARTY

| Martin, William | 555-0304 |
| OPPOSING COUNSEL | TELEPHONE |

	FILE TAB	1
	CLIENT FILE	2
	ADVERSE PARTY	3
	SEC'Y TICKLER CLIENT	4
	SEC'Y TICKLER ADVERSE	5

A legal secretary might use this form with carbons for reference information to be placed in various files, as indicated at the bottom of each copy. The first form is attached to the client folder so that the top part serves as a folder tab.

TYPES OF CARD FILES

Card records may be stored in *vertical* card files or in *visible* card files (frequently referred to simply as *visible files*).

In vertical card files, cards stand upright in file drawers, like correspondence. In visible files, cards are stored in such a way that information may be read without handling the cards. The illustration at the top of page 71 shows information recorded on a card stored in a vertical file and a card stored in a visible file.

VERTICAL CARD FILES. Vertical card files do not require folders to hold the cards because each card is an independent record that contains information about one name, address, location, topic, or product. In addition, cards are relatively heavy, do not curl, and therefore stand vertically in the file without much support.

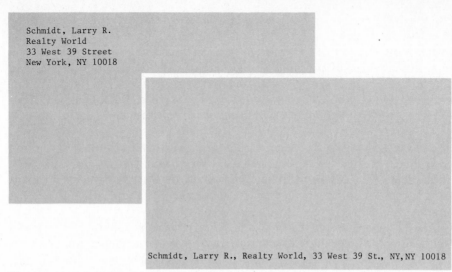

Schmidt, Larry R.
Realty World
33 West 39 Street
New York, NY 10018

Schmidt, Larry R., Realty World, 33 West 39 St., NY,NY 10018

The top card is for use in vertical files; the bottom, for use in visible files.

Standard Card Sizes. Standard sizes for cards are 5 by 3 inches, 6 by 4 inches, and 8 by 5 inches (the first dimension given is the side on which the card rests when stored). The dimensions of the punched cards that are used to store and process information by computers is 7 3/8 by 3 1/4 inches.

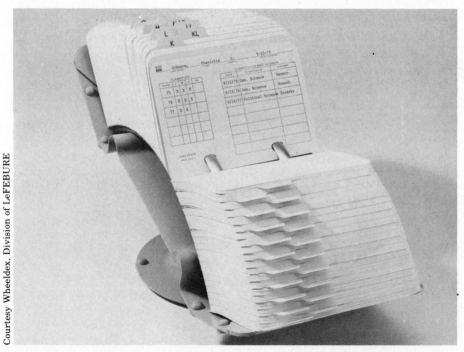

Courtesy Wheeldex, Division of LeFEBURE

The administrative office of a school might use posted card records to maintain up-to-date data on students enrolled at the school.

The size of card selected (unless it is to be machine processed, in which case you need to use the size required by the equipment) will depend on its use and the amount of information to be recorded on the card. Cards used to record names and addresses of individuals need only be 5 by 3 inches to provide adequate space. A card used to record health examination information, however, would normally need to be 8 by 5 inches, using both sides to record all the necessary information in a compact format.

Information Placement.   When cards are prepared for storing, the caption should be typed on the second line from the top of the card. All other key data should be as close to the caption as possible so that the card can be read without being removed from its container.

Guides.   Regardless of the size of the cards, there should be one guide in the file drawer for each twenty-five to fifty cards. For faster finding, vertical card files that are frequently referred to should have one guide for each twenty-five cards. In some vertical card files, in addition to the guides, each card has its own tab, usually bearing a number. This greatly speeds up finding when cards are constantly being removed from and inserted into the file. In most card systems, though, the cards have no tabs.

VISIBLE CARD FILES.   A great many types of visible card files are available: (1) horizontal trays, (2) vertical racks, (3) open bins or tubs, (4) rotary wheels, and (5) loose-leaf visible books. All of these types have an important feature in common, and it is from this feature that visible files get their name: *key information on each record can be seen without handling when*

Each of the two wheels on this motorized card file holds 5,000 cards.

the record is in storage because the information is on a projecting edge. Thus visible files are used when it is essential that information be found rapidly. For incoming calls, the telephone operator of a company might use a visible file to find extension numbers quickly so that important customers would be talking to executives in a matter of seconds.

Visible files for posted records, such as inventories, are easy to keep up to date. With a drawer-type horizontal file tray, new inventory facts can be quickly posted or handwritten on the card. In addition, the card never has to be removed from its holder.

The requirements of the organization as to volume, location, portability, and use should determine the type of visible file to be used. Horizontal trays are well suited for posted visible records. Vertical racks are handy for quick reference to names, code numbers, and telephone numbers, while bins or tubs make excellent containers for machine-posted records. Rotary wheels provide fast reference to such information as addresses and credit data; and loose-leaf visible books, because they are portable, provide a quick reference to product information for traveling salespersons.

Standard Card Sizes.   Cards for visible card files are similar to those used for vertical card files. The difference in the two types lies in the arrangement of the information on the cards.

Information Placement.   Placement of the information to be typed or printed on visible cards will be determined by the arrangement of the file.

A visible file such as this one allows the worker to quickly find the desired card by reading the visible index on each card. It is set up with counter space for manual posting of information.

When visible record cards are being prepared, the caption should be typed as close as possible to the visible edge. Because the cards are often stored with their edges overlapping, the file worker should be certain that the caption is not obscured by another card.

Guides. Guides are not used in most visible files because each acts as its own guide. But certain facts, such as the quantity of a product on hand, can be made to stand out by using signals—colored plastic or paper strips, tabs, or clips that can be placed on the visible portion of a card. The position or color of the signals can be used to classify, schedule, and follow up such records as inventory, sales, accounts receivable, and accounts payable.

BUSINESS FORMS

Business forms are documents with blanks or spaces for the insertion of requested information. They are used in offices to record and process information of a repetitive nature in an efficient way.

Forms are important carriers of business information and are the most frequently used record in the majority of offices. Forms may be printed on paper of approximately the same weight and size as that used for correspondence, or they may be printed on cards.

TYPES OF INFORMATION RECORDED ON FORMS. Every business form has information printed on it and space for information to be added.

Printed Guide Words. The information which is already printed on the form is called static information. Examples are *pay to the order of, ship to, sold to, name, address,* and *telephone.*

Variable Information. The information which is added to the forms in the blank spaces is called *variable information* because it may change with each form. A good example might be the address goods are shipped to. When you complete a form, you are supplying variable information. Variable information may also be referred to as *fill-in information* or *fill-ins.*

PURPOSES OF BUSINESS FORMS

The forms used in business systems serve three basic purposes.

SOURCE OF INPUT. Every business transaction must have a beginning. The original record of a business event is made on some type of business record, and this original record is known as a *source document* or *source record.* For example, the original record for a weekly payroll is usually made on a time card for each employee. Each of these source records is a means for putting information into the business system; hence the term *input* is used to describe their purpose.

MEANS OF PROCESSING INFORMATION. The purpose of a business system is to process, or change the form of, input data so that the information will

DATE October 12, 19--	PHONE RES. 555-3858			PHONE BUS. 555-1122						

1. John T. Magruder

2.

ADDRESS 1368 West Avenue, New York, NY 10025

STS	FROM	TO	CARR.	FLIGHT	CL.	DATE/DAY	LEAVE	ARRIVE	STATUS	OPTION	CONFIRMED DATE/BY	FARES	
	RIC	LAG	PI	501	Y	11/3/-- Wed	8:01A	9:06A			10/12 rk	66	00
	LAG	RIC	PI	502	Y	11/5/-- Fri	10:40P	11:45P				66	00

HOTEL RESERVATIONS	DATE IN	DATE OUT	NO. OF NIGHTS	RATE	TYPE	TOTAL	COMM.
New York Hotel	11/3	11/5	2	51.00	single	102.00	
MISCELLANEOUS							
TRANSPORTATION						132.00	
					TOTAL	234.00	
					TAXES		
					TOTAL	234.00	
					DEPOSIT		
					BALANCE		
					PAID ON	11/2--	

This form serves as input since information on it is used to prepare tickets and an itinerary. Since data on it is used to process information, it also serves as an intermediate record. Front (above) and back of the card are shown.

be useful in the operation of the business. Processing operations include such activities as classifying, sorting, computing, recording, summarizing, and storing.

Information can be processed both manually and automatically. Three methods of processing information automatically that are commonly used in the business world are:

1. The equipment used by banks to process checks by means of Magnetic Ink Character Recognition (MICR) can also be used by business for processing card records.
2. Punched cards can be read by machines, and many businesses use this format for billing and inventory purposes.
3. Cards marked with special pencils can be read by optical scanning devices for computer processing.

Billing Date	Plus Current Charges
12-04---	42.30

GEO   Great Eastern Oil Company
127 Hartsdale Avenue, Dover, DE 19901

Previous Balance	Plus Installments
38.50	Install Conv Amount

Less Payments
38.50

Account Number
2637322765

Less Credits

JAMES F. MACDONALD
128 HAWLEY ROAD
LATROBE, PA 15650

Past Due Balance

New Balance
42.30

Payment due upon receipt of statement

Plus FINANCE CHARGE   New Balance
42.30

Return this portion with your payment

To avoid additional FINANCE CHARGE, new balance must be
paid within 25 days after billing date except under extended
payment arrangements as explained on reverse side.

If Not A Credit
Pay This Total

Indicate change of
address on re-
turn envelope by
checking box

FINANCE CHARGE SCHEDULE

Unpaid Balance	Periodic Rate Per Month	ANNUAL PERCENTAGE RATE
To $ 500	1-1/2%	18 %
Over $ 500	1%	12 %

Account Number
1 2637322765

2637322765

This card serves three purposes: to bill the customer; to provide a receipt
for the customer; to provide a record of payment by the customer. It is
an example of an action record.

MEANS OF OUTPUT.   The results of processing are of value to the business
only when they have been communicated to the proper persons for action.
Processed data transmitted out of a system is referred to as *output*. Records
that are used to report output data are *action records*. For example, the
keeping of a customer's account, an intermediate record, is of no value to
a business unless the customer eventually pays his debt. The monthly
statement, which ideally causes the customer to pay, is an action record in
a sales system.

Many systems within businesses use cards and forms to process information. Purchases and accounts payable systems assure that merchandise
for resale or raw materials are obtained and that payment is made for them
at the proper time. Shipping and receiving records ensure that outgoing
products are sent promptly and economically and that incoming materials
are efficiently received, checked, and delivered to the using department.
Cash records ensure proper control of money received and paid by the
business. Inventory records provide information for deciding what items
need to be purchased in order to keep the stock of materials or merchandise
at a satisfactory level.

The chart on page 77 shows how certain forms serve business purposes.

SURVEY OF COMPETENCIES

GENERAL REVIEW

The following questions will help you to reinforce your learning of the
competencies included in this chapter.

1.   What are card records? Name three examples of card records.   (Competency 1)
2.   What are the advantages of using card records?   (Competency 1)

Source records:
  W-4 Forms (Employee's Withholding
      Exemption Certificates)
  Salary and wage schedules from personnel department
  Payroll change reports from personnel department
  Incoming punched time cards for hourly employees

Intermediate records:
  Payroll register or journal
  Employee earnings records
  Currency breakdown for cash payroll

Action records:
  Check and voucher or pay envelope to employees
  Blank time cards to check-in stations
  Reports for government, such as:
    Federal Depositary Receipt (Form 450)
    Employer's Quarterly Federal Tax Return (Form 941)
    Wage and Tax Statement (Form W-2)

The purposes of payroll records are to assemble data for the payment of employees and to provide information for tax reports to the federal, state, and local governments.

3. Name and describe the two categories of card records. (Competency 2)
4. What are three commonly used sizes of card records? What will determine the size selected for use? (Competency 2)
5. Compare and contrast vertical and visible files. (Competency 3)
6. State what is meant by printed guide words and variable information on business forms. (Competency 4)
7. State three purposes of business forms. (Competency 5)
8. Name three forms and describe how each is used by a business. (Competency 5)

CASE PROBLEMS

1. Longview Community Hospital uses a card index at its reception desk to supply information about the room locations of the patients. Currently the hospital uses a card index contained in a metal drawer-type file. The receptionist must go through the cards and pull out the one needed. From what you have learned in this chapter, what would be a better system of locating patients? In addition, the hospital would like to determine at a glance which patients are allowed visitors during general visiting hours and which patients have restricted visiting hours. Can you suggest a method which would help? Why would a card index be helpful for this kind of information instead of a list or other format?   (Competencies 1, 2, 3)

2. Charlotte Adams has been hired to fill a new position as office manager at the XYZ Co. One of the responsibilities she must assume is suggesting ways to make the files better serve the needs of the office staff. She discovered that no card files were used; all papers were housed in centrally located correspondence file cabinets. She recommended the purchase of card files and suggested five instances in which card files would save time for the employees. What are your ideas about when card files would be more efficient than correspondence files?   (Competencies 1, 2, 3)

3. Business forms and cards are found in many places. Think of the different forms or cards that you have seen; classify each as a source of input, output, or an intermediate record. Name three source documents that you or someone you know has generated in the business community recently.   (Competency 5)

4. Some stores record their inventory on cards using a separate card for each item. Why are cards used instead of lists? Can any information be printed on the cards prior to inventory?   (Competencies 1, 2, 3, 4, 5)

5. John Rogers uses forms in the office where he works. He feels that it would be just as easy to jot down the information he needs and eliminate the form. Do you agree with him?   (Competencies 4, 5)

If you have not mastered all of the competencies reviewed in the Survey, reread that part of the chapter which deals with the competency in question; then recheck your progress.

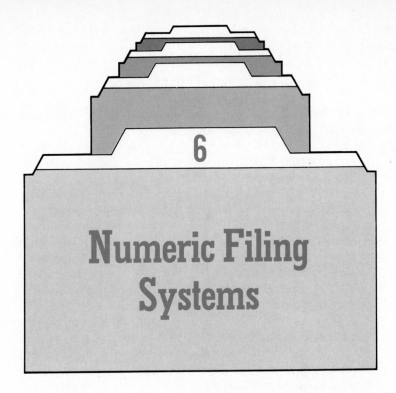

6

Numeric Filing Systems

When you have completed this chapter, you will be able to:

1. Define numeric filing.
2. State the advantages of numeric filing.
3. List and describe the parts of a numeric filing system.
4. File and find cards using a consecutive numeric filing system. (See Jobs 23 to 25 in the *Practice Materials.*)
5. File and find cards using a terminal-digit filing system. (See Jobs 26 to 28 in the *Practice Materials.*)
6. File and find cards using a middle-digit filing system. (See Jobs 29 to 31 in the *Practice Materials.*)
7. Index and code correspondence for filing, prepare cross-references, and file and find correspondence using a numeric system. (See Jobs 32 to 36 in the *Practice Materials.*)
8. Explain the procedure for transferring papers from a miscellaneous alphabetic file to a numeric file.

NUMERIC FILING

Numeric filing is the most common method of filing for large groups where alphabetizing of all the many names and keeping them in order would be difficult. Think, for example, of the millions of contributors to social security; think of all the major credit card owners and automobile license owners. The only efficient way to keep those records in order is to file them by number.

DEFINITION OF NUMERIC FILING. Numeric filing is the arrangement of records according to numbers. The number may be assigned to the record, or it may be a part of the record itself (such as the number that appears on an invoice or a check). Filing records in consecutive order according to these numbers is called *consecutive* or *serial* numeric filing. Other methods of arranging records numerically are discussed later in this chapter.

Numeric filing systems are called *indirect systems* because you must first consult an alphabetic index to determine the code number of a record. Alphabetic filing systems, on the other hand, are *direct systems* because you can go directly to the file drawer and, by means of the name captions, find the records for which you are searching.

For example, in numeric files, a letter from Alice Johnson would be filed in a folder with an assigned number such as *82-3368* (as might be the case in a lawyer's office) or by *533 678 9923 003 442* (which might be a charge account number) or by *98-6655-4321-448* (which might be an insurance policy number). Therefore, it is necessary to understand the basis for the numeric filing system before you can determine where the record should be stored and why it should be stored in that particular location.

In an alphabetic system the letter would be filed in a folder labeled *J* or *Johnson*.

ADVANTAGE OF NUMERIC FILING. Numeric filing systems have six advantages over alphabetic, subject, and geographic systems, as follows.

Sequential Identification of Records. Records that have been identified by number are easy to put in sequential order. Although the process of identifying the record can take time, as you will see later in this chapter, once the number has been assigned, the filing process is speeded up. Names can be similar, even identical, which can cause confusion; numbers assigned according to an established pattern are always different.

Convenient Expansion. Because numeric filing systems allow for the addition of numbers as the need arises, expansion is easier than with alphabetic systems. Additional folders and, as necessary, additional storage units can be added without moving any files. In an alphabetic system, if you needed more room in the *A* drawer, you would need to move the folders in all drawers to expand at the beginning.

Permanent and Extensive Cross-Referencing. Some businesses, such as law firms and contractors, deal with records that refer to definite cases, contracts, or operations that are active for relatively long and indefinite periods. Because each case, contract, or operation usually refers to several names or several other cases, an extensive cross-reference is necessary. This can be provided in the card index of a numeric file.

Card Index as an Integral Part of the System. The card index used for locating the assigned number for a correspondent can also be used for other purposes by the business. For example, it provides a list of names, addresses, and telephone numbers; a quick reference check to see if there is a file already for the customer; a reference to previous business which may have been transacted or is in progress; credit information; the names of persons to contact about various matters, such as the head of the marketing division, the accounting department, or the repair service. In short, the card index can be as useful to you as you care to make it.

Confidentiality of Information. Because the files are referred to by number, and numbers are impersonal, there is less temptation to "snoop" in the files. All alphabetic references to files are contained only in the card index. If you meet a stranger in the hall while carrying files with only numbers, no conclusions can be reached. However, if that individual saw you carrying files about James R. Sinclair and Herman G. Overton, the conclusion could be reached, and correctly, that your employer had important business dealings with those individuals. The stranger might gain an advantage from having that knowledge.

Making Use of a Number Already an Identifying Factor. There are many instances when a number is already the means of identification, such as social security numbers, telephone numbers, invoice numbers, and charge account numbers. Particularly if the information to be filed could be (or some day will be) stored in a computer, it makes sense to use a number already available. As an easy numeric system, a store may file telephone orders according to the last digit of the telephone number. This divides them evenly into ten groups. The customer's last name is used to file within each group. For example, Robert Denton's invoice would be filed in folder 3 since his telephone number is 512-555-6863. Within the folder his invoice would be filed between an invoice for Joseph Decker and one for Arnold Denver.

Social security numbers are used by many businesses and institutions for identification of individuals. This is a unique means of identification and one that most people easily remember.

NUMERIC CARD FILES

Numbers are used to standardize caption size and arrangement, which is especially important if information is to be recorded in a limited space, on a 5 by 3 card, for example, or in a computer's memory where access to a specific location is important. Numbers are also unique identifiers of records; two people can have identical names, but they cannot have identical

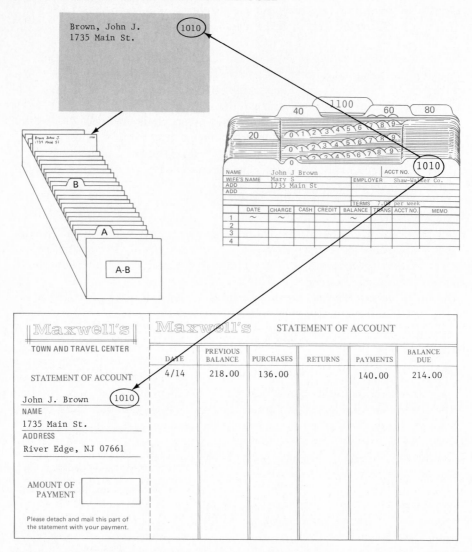

The numeric card file for customer account cards (upper right) is the source file for the preparation of the monthly statement shown at the bottom. The card file at the upper left is an alphabetic index to customer account numbers.

social security numbers. Generally an identification number will be shorter than a name. A vendor number of five or six digits can be used for processing sales records rather than writing out the name of the vendor each time. Office workers find that sorting cards by number is faster than sorting by names. An example of a numeric card filing system is shown above.

In card files, guides are used to divide the cards into workable groups. For example, a file of 100 cards would probably be divided into groups of 10 for easy reference, with the guides 00, 10, 20, 30, 40, 50, 60, 70, 80, and 90.

OTHER NUMERIC CARD SYSTEMS

In addition to the consecutive, or serial, type, other numeric systems used in business are (1) terminal-digit systems, (2) triple-digit systems, (3) middle-digit systems, and (4) duplex-numeric systems.

In *terminal-digit* systems the numbers are read from right to left. The numbers are generally analyzed in three parts. The last, or terminal, two digits are the drawer number, the next two digits are the folder number, and all the other digits indicate the sequence in the folder. To illustrate, an insurance policy numbered 421597 would be stored in the drawer numbered 97 (last two digits) and in the folder numbered 15 (middle two digits), and the 42 (first two digits) would determine its sequence in the folder.

COMPARISON OF CONSECUTIVE-NUMERIC AND
TERMINAL-DIGIT SYSTEMS

If you were filing business forms
bearing these numbers:

23753
23747
23750
23752
23756
23755

1. In a consecutive numeric system, they would all be filed in numeric order in one drawer (starred).

2. In a terminal-digit system, the numbers would first be broken into these groups:

2	37	47
2	37	50
2	37	52
2	37	53
2	37	55
2	37	56
Sequence in folder	Folder number	Drawer number

Reading the numbers from right to left, you would then file the forms first by drawer number, then by folder number, and finally by sequence within the folder. Thus the six forms would be stored in six separate file drawers in folder number 37.

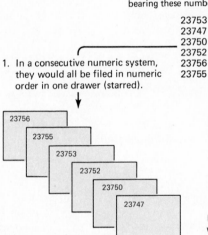

000	20000*	40000
5000	25000	45000
10000	30000	50000
15000	35000	55000

45	49	53*
46	50*	54
47*	51	55*
48	52*	56*

When many forms have to be filed by several file workers, the terminal-digit system is an advantage because it overcomes crowded working conditions by spreading the work over several file drawers.

Terminal-digit systems have the advantages of an even distribution of records in the files at all times and permanent numbering of cabinets and primary guides, even after records have been transferred. The illustration on page 83 compares consecutive-numeric and terminal-digit systems.

Triple-digit systems are similar to terminal-digit systems except that the numbers are broken into two parts, instead of three. The last three digits of a number on the extreme right are called *primary numbers,* and the remaining digits determine the sequence of records in the folder bearing the primary numbers. For example, Insurance Policy No. 421597 would be stored in Folder 597. The 421 would determine its sequence in the folder.

In *middle-digit* systems (sometimes called *significant-number systems*), records are separated first according to the third and fourth digits from the right of a number, then according to the first two digits on the left, and finally according to the last two digits on the right. For example, Insurance Policy No. 421597 would be stored in Drawer 15 (middle two digits), and in Folder 42 (first two digits). The 97 would determine its sequence in the folder.

Duplex-numeric systems use digits and letters of the alphabet, separated by hyphens or commas, to code records numerically. In Chapter 7 there is a further discussion of this system.

FILING PRACTICE

You are now ready to complete Jobs 23 to 25 (consecutive numeric filing), Jobs 26 to 28 (terminal digit filing), and Jobs 29 to 31 (middle digit filing) of the *Practice Materials.*

NUMERIC CORRESPONDENCE FILING

Numeric correspondence filing is used when the records to be stored will be requested by number, when they would be difficult to classify under one particular name, when confidentiality is facilitated by using numbers for identification, and when rapid expansion of the files may be necessary. Lawyers and businesses which deal in contract work often file by number.

ORGANIZATION OF A NUMERIC CORRESPONDENCE FILE. A numeric correspondence file has four parts: (1) main numeric file, (2) miscellaneous alphabetic file, (3) card index, and (4) register for determining the next number to be assigned.

Main Numeric File. The main numeric file contains guides and individual folders that bear numeric captions. Each numbered folder contains records concerning a separate correspondent. As in alphabetic filing, the records within the folder are arranged chronologically with the most recent date on top.

There is a numeric guide for each group of five to ten folders. The guides may be arranged in one of three ways:

1. The guide tabs may be in three positions staggered from left to right.
2. The guide tabs may appear in two or more positions on the left with the folder tabs in the last position to the right.
3. The guide tabs may be in the center only, and the folder tabs may be in two positions to the left and two positions to the right.

Guide tabs are numbered in fives or tens unless the contents of each folder contain ten numbers, in which case the guides are numbered in hundreds.

When a numeric folder becomes full, the records can be subdivided by date or subject, depending on how they will be requested. When the records are subdivided and half of them are placed in a new folder, both the new and the old folder bear the same caption as the old one, plus an auxiliary number. The auxiliary number gives further identification—for example, Folder 206 upon being subdivided becomes 206-2 and the new folder is 206-1. This is illustrated at the bottom of this page.

Miscellaneous Alphabetic File.   The miscellaneous alphabetic file contains guides and folders bearing alphabetic captions. Its purpose is to provide a place to store pieces of correspondence that do not warrant individual folders in the main numeric file. Therefore, every folder in this file is a miscellaneous folder containing the records of several correspondents. Rec-

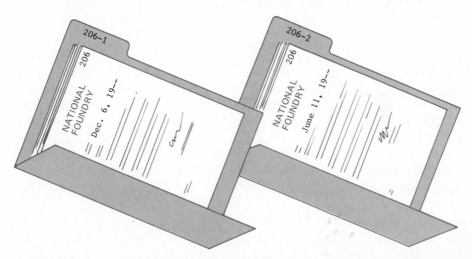

To prevent overcrowding, these numeric folders have been subdivided by date. When enough papers are stored to warrant opening a new folder, the new folder is numbered 206-1—and the existing folder is renumbered 206-2—so that the most recent papers are in the first folder. If another folder is needed, 206-1 then becomes 206-2, 206-2 becomes 206-3, and so on.

ords, of course, proceed in strict alphabetic order throughout the file. When five or more records concerning one correspondent accumulate, they are assigned the next unused number, placed in a numeric folder corresponding to this number, and stored in the main numeric file.

The miscellaneous alphabetic file can be in the front of the first drawer of the main numeric file, in a separate drawer of the main numeric file, or in a separate filing cabinet.

Card Index.   The card index, arranged alphabetically, contains cards, each with the name (and usually the address and other information) of a correspondent, together with the number assigned to the records of that correspondent. This type of index is necessary in all numeric correspondence systems because correspondence is usually called for by name rather than by number. If the records are kept in the miscellaneous alphabetic file, this is indicated on the card by the symbol *M*. The *M* is eliminated and a folder number is written in its place when the correspondent is assigned a folder in the main numeric file.

Register.   The register shows the names and numbers already assigned and the numbers available. When a new correspondent warrants an individual folder, the register is consulted and the next available number is assigned. If any correspondence has been placed in the miscellaneous alphabetic file, it is removed, coded with the assigned number, and placed in proper sequence in the folder. The card in the card index is updated to show the assigned number. In some systems, when the file for that particular correspondent is no longer needed, it may be removed from the files and destroyed. The number may then be assigned to another folder.

CROSS-REFERENCING.   You will recall that cross-referencing in alphabetic systems is accomplished by placing cross-reference sheets or copies of the original document in the individual and miscellaneous folders. In numeric filing systems, however, cross-referencing is done in the card index. This was discussed at the beginning of the chapter as an advantage of numeric filing systems.

For example, the letter illustrated on page 87 deals with a change of billing procedure. A card made up for Imports Limited will contain a notation concerning this company's relationship with Alexander Imports Inc.

STEPS IN NUMERIC CORRESPONDENCE FILING.   The steps in numeric correspondence filing are inspecting, alphabetic indexing and coding, alphabetic sorting, numeric coding, numeric sorting, and storing. A diagram of this process is shown on page 88.

Inspecting.   As in alphabetic correspondence filing, the correspondence is checked for a release mark before filing.

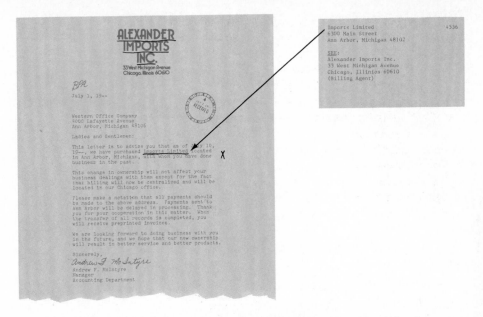

Since records regarding Imports Limited are now filed under *Alexander Imports,* a cross-reference card in the card index is needed to lead the file worker to the proper folder.

Alphabetic Indexing and Coding.   Alphabetic indexing and coding are the same as for alphabetic card filing (see Chapters 2 and 3).

Alphabetic Sorting.   The correspondence to be filed is sorted into alphabetic order so that the card index can be consulted to code each piece with the proper number. This step is necessary only the first time a record is filed. After that, because the number has been written on the paper, you can skip all steps up to the numeric sorting.

Numeric Coding.   The card index is consulted for each piece of correspondence. The number is written on the record, usually in the upper right-hand corner. If there is no number assigned, the record is coded with the letter *M* to indicate that it is to be stored in the miscellaneous alphabetic file.

Numeric Sorting.   After the numeric coding is finished, the papers are sorted into numeric order. As in alphabetic filing, you should use rough and fine sorting techniques. The number of piles will depend on the range of numbers with which you need to work, but four to six will fit conveniently on most desk tops.

Storing.   The papers are then placed in the proper place in their files in the file drawers as in alphabetic filing.

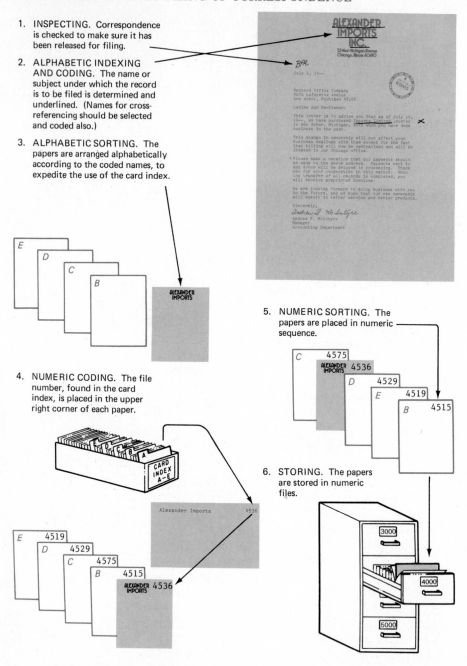

1. INSPECTING. Correspondence is checked to make sure it has been released for filing.

2. ALPHABETIC INDEXING AND CODING. The name or subject under which the record is to be filed is determined and underlined. (Names for cross-referencing should be selected and coded also.)

3. ALPHABETIC SORTING. The papers are arranged alphabetically according to the coded names, to expedite the use of the card index.

4. NUMERIC CODING. The file number, found in the card index, is placed in the upper right corner of each paper.

5. NUMERIC SORTING. The papers are placed in numeric sequence.

6. STORING. The papers are stored in numeric files.

USING A MISCELLANEOUS ALPHABETIC FILE WITH A NUMERIC FILE. In the illustration on page 89, incoming letters were coded with a number that was found in the card index. Then the letters were stored in correct order according to number. A numeric file only was used.

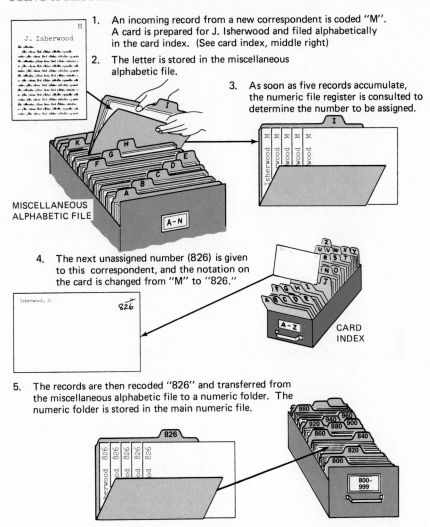

1. An incoming record from a new correspondent is coded "M". A card is prepared for J. Isherwood and filed alphabetically in the card index. (See card index, middle right)

2. The letter is stored in the miscellaneous alphabetic file.

3. As soon as five records accumulate, the numeric file register is consulted to determine the number to be assigned.

MISCELLANEOUS ALPHABETIC FILE

4. The next unassigned number (826) is given to this correspondent, and the notation on the card is changed from "M" to "826."

CARD INDEX

5. The records are then recoded "826" and transferred from the miscellaneous alphabetic file to a numeric folder. The numeric folder is stored in the main numeric file.

Some offices use a combination of a miscellaneous alphabetic file with a numeric file. In the miscellaneous alphabetic file, papers from correspondents are stored until at least five records are accumulated from a correspondent. Then the papers are transferred to the numeric system. The illustration above explains the process of transferring papers from a miscellaneous alphabetic file to a numeric file.

FILING PRACTICE

You are now ready to complete Jobs 32 to 36 of the *Practice Materials*.

SURVEY OF COMPETENCIES

GENERAL REVIEW

You have had an opportunity to put into practice much of the material you have learned in this chapter. There are a few points, however, that you need to review to reinforce your competencies.

1. What is numeric filing? (Competency 1)
2. What are six advantages of numeric filing? (Competency 2)
3. List and describe the parts of a numeric filing system. (Competency 3)
4. What is meant by *consecutive numeric? Terminal-digit? Middle-digit?* (Competencies 4, 5, 6)
5. What are the steps in preparing correspondence to be filed numerically? (Competency 7)
6. How is cross-referencing done in numeric filing systems? (Competencies 2, 7)
7. When and how is a folder changed from the miscellaneous alphabetic file to the numeric file? (Competency 8)

CASE PROBLEMS

1. Your supervisor, Gerald Linder, does not think that it is necessary to maintain a card index for your numeric files. He feels that the register will provide you with all the necessary information to assign numbers to the daily correspondence. Is this feasible? How are you going to convince him? (Competencies 2, 3)
2. Your predecessor cross-referenced information in the main numeric file, or not at all. This is very frustrating for you since you have to go to several files to find what you are looking for. You would like to cross-reference the card index. Should you change the present system? If so, what should you do about cross-references already in the files? (Competencies 2, 3, 7)
3. Your employer is currently using an alphabetic filing system. You find there are problems with the system and you think a numeric system would solve them. Some of the problems are:

   a. Overcrowding in the file drawers. As the number of folders in each drawer increases, you have been taking several file folders from the back of the crowded drawers and moving them to an empty drawer. You have not had the time to redistribute the file folders in all the drawers to keep them in alphabetic order. Thus you have two groups of folders which need to be checked each time you file records.

   b. Difficulty in locating files which contain records about a project and which involve three or four individuals. Currently the records are filed under the name of one of the individuals.

c. Slowness in retrieving information. Many orders come in over the telephone and you rush to the files to find out whether the potential customer has an acceptable credit standing and the limit of credit allowable. Also you want to know whether the customer is a new one or has submitted previous orders.

d. Mistakes in vendor numbers. Each large-volume customer has a vendor number assigned, and you use it for identification on several forms instead of the name. Customers with small volume, however, do not have numbers; usually these are one- or two-time orders which do not need to be kept in the files with customers with large businesses who may have more than one file.

What advantages would numeric filing have over your present system? How are you going to convince your employer that a change would be a more efficient filing method? (Competencies 2, 3)

If you have not mastered all of the competencies reviewed in the Survey, reread that part of the chapter which deals with the competency in question; then recheck your progress.

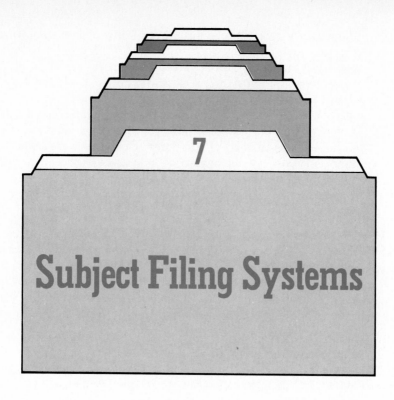

Subject Filing Systems

When you have completed this chapter, you will be able to:

1. Define subject filing.
2. State the advantages of subject filing and give examples of business situations in which subject filing is used.
3. List and describe the parts of a subject correspondence file.
4. File and find cards using a subject filing system. (See Jobs 37 to 40 in the *Practice Materials*.)
5. Index and code correspondence for filing, prepare cross-references, and file and find correspondence using a subject system. (See Jobs 41 to 45 in the *Practice Materials*.)
6. Describe the three kinds of subject filing systems.
7. Describe chronological filing and set up a chronological file. (See Job 46 in the *Practice Materials*.)
8. Organize a list of folder captions into a dictionary arrangement and then reorganize them into an encyclopedic arrangement.
9. Select guide and folder captions when given a list of items which are to be filed using a subject system.

SUBJECT FILING

Subject filing is the arrangement of records by names of items or topics rather than by names of people, companies, or locations. In subject filing, records related to one subject or area of business activity may be grouped and stored in one place to provide a complete picture of what has transpired on the subject.

ARRANGEMENT OF SUBJECT FILE DRAWER.   The subject file drawer is arranged in the same way as the alphabetic file drawer: The captions determine which system is being used. In alphabetic filing the captions are the names of people or organizations; in subject filing the captions are names of items, objects, or business activities or functions. Examples of subject captions in a bookstore are *Inventory Control, Personnel Policies, Purchase Requisitions, Textbook Orders,* and *Trucking Rates.*

SUBJECT FILING USED WITH OTHER SYSTEMS.   Some records, such as inventory cards, are referred to only by the name of the item, and thus they are filed by subject only. Other records, such as insurance policies, have a policyholder's name, a policy number, and a subject (*Insurance Policies*) and may be filed in any of the three ways. It is important to remember that any filing system has to be adjusted to fit the needs of a particular office. An office may choose to adapt any one system or use a combination of systems if that is the way the office wants to organize its records.

SUBJECT FILING AS A MEANS OF ORGANIZING RELATED RECORDS.   In subject filing, a common element is identified under which several or many papers may be grouped. Such a grouping helps to organize those records and make them easy to find. Following are examples of this application of subject filing.

Information on the care and maintenance of a piece of new equipment, such as a typewriter, would probably be stored under the subject *EQUIP-MENT REPAIR: Typewriter.* Thus you would not have folders for maintenance of each type of equipment used in the office scattered throughout the files; they would all be behind the guide *EQUIPMENT REPAIR.*

Records relating to the construction of a new building would be stored in one place—probably the name of the building or site location. Thus papers from many different sources related to that construction—such as different subcontractors—would be grouped in one logical place for reference.

A hotel would probably file contracts for meetings scheduled for the month of November behind a guide labeled *BOOKINGS: NOVEMBER* so that all the commitments for that month would be in one place as a help in planning the overall operation of the hotel's meeting facilities.

SUBJECT CARD FILING

Subject card filing serves the same purposes as alphabetic card filing: as an index to complete files or as a handy reference for information that is frequently needed.

The subject card catalog in the library is helpful to use when you do not know either the name of an author or the title of a book to help you find the information you want. So, too, in an office there are kinds of information you need in your day-to-day activities which are best organized by subject. Many offices have card files which list items such as repair service for machines, emergency telephone numbers, departments in the organization with the name and extension of the individual who can best handle certain matters, and an agenda showing regularly scheduled activities for each month of the year.

Guides in subject card files are the same as guides used in alphabetic card files; however, the captions are subjects rather than names.

SUBJECT CORRESPONDENCE FILING

ORGANIZATION OF SUBJECT CORRESPONDENCE FILES. A subject correspondence file has two parts—main subject file and relative index. If there are only a few folders with subject captions, they may be filed in alphabetic order in the same drawers as the alphabetic correspondence folders.

Main Subject File. The main subject file contains guides and folders that bear subject captions. The hardest task when setting up a subject file is determining parallel captions to use in the filing system. For example, you would not have guide captions such as *Office Supplies, Typing Paper, Annual Report, Annual Report for 1981,* and *Annual Report Design Award* in the same file. You need to select parallel captions. Instead of these, you would have as a guide caption *OFFICE SUPPLIES,* and then you would subdivide that subject into the following folder captions: *OFFICE SUPPLIES: Typing Paper; OFFICE SUPPLIES: Memos; OFFICE SUPPLIES: Letterheads;* and so on. You would also have as a guide *ANNUAL REPORT,* then subdivide that subject according to year, such as *ANNUAL REPORT: 1981; ANNUAL REPORT: 1980; ANNUAL REPORT: Design Award;* and so on.

Each guide caption should be of equal importance and of a broad enough description that it may be subdivided as necessary. As a general rule, you should outline the headings for a subject filing system as you would outline the topics and subtopics of an English composition.

Relative Index. People do not all reason the same way, and therefore what one person considers the main subject may not be the same as what another person thinks. It may depend on a particular person's interest in the subject. For example, a staff member who wants to compete for a design award for the cover of the annual report may think the logical place to file information on the award is under *ART DEPARTMENT* or *PUBLIC RELATIONS,* whereas the information was filed under *ANNUAL REPORT.*

To take care of a situation where different guide captions might be referred to, subject files need a relative index. This listing tells what the main headings, divisions, and subdivisions are. This listing will not only help you find the right folder, but also guide you in the selection of the subject caption for new items to be filed. It serves the same purpose as the index of a book. There is much decision making in subject filing; therefore, the person who sets up guide and folder captions should be knowledgeable about the business and the manner in which files are requested.

CROSS-REFERENCING.   Cross-referencing is done in the relative index in the same way information is cross-referenced in the index of a book. For example, the entry *Design Award* might be followed by *See Annual Report.* This will be explained in more detail in the discussion of alphabetic subject files.

KINDS OF SUBJECT CORRESPONDENCE FILES.   The principal kinds of subject files are combination subject, alphabetic subject, and numeric subject.

Combination Subject Files.   A combination subject file contains subject captions mixed in with individual or company name captions. This kind of subject file is used when there is relatively little material to be organized on a subject basis. In such a case it is impractical to set up a separate subject file, and so the subject captions, as described earlier in this chapter, are merged with name captions in what would otherwise be an alphabetic correspondence file. Combination subject files are illustrated on this page and on page 96.

Alphabetic Subject Files.   Alphabetic subject files are similar to alphabetic correspondence files except that all the captions refer to topics instead of

COMBINATION SUBJECT FILE

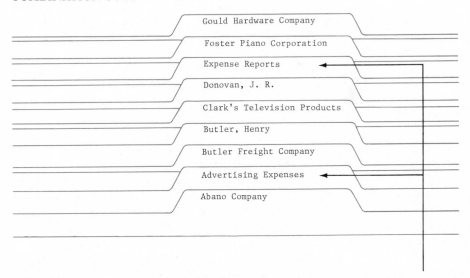

Arrows point to subject folders interfiled with folders for individual and company names.

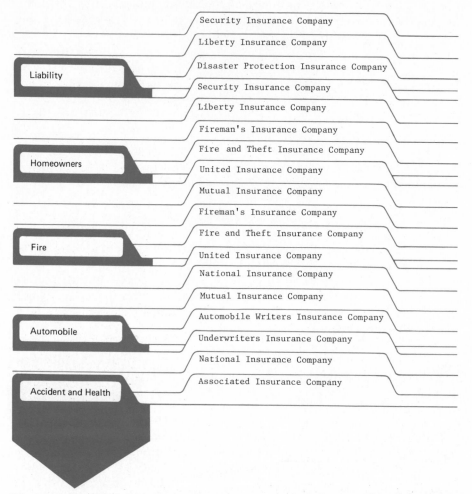

Security Insurance Company

Liberty Insurance Company

Disaster Protection Insurance Company

Liability

Security Insurance Company

Liberty Insurance Company

Fireman's Insurance Company

Fire and Theft Insurance Company

Homeowners

United Insurance Company

Mutual Insurance Company

Fireman's Insurance Company

Fire and Theft Insurance Company

Fire

United Insurance Company

National Insurance Company

Mutual Insurance Company

Automobile Writers Insurance Company

Automobile

Underwriters Insurance Company

National Insurance Company

Associated Insurance Company

Accident and Health

Here is another example of a combination subject file in which main headings are subjects and subheadings are company names. An insurance agency might file forms for new policies first by the type of policy and then by the names of the companies whose policies they write.

people and organizations. There are two arrangements for alphabetic subject files—encyclopedic and dictionary.

A subject file with *encyclopedic arrangement* has alphabetized major headings, which in turn have alphabetized divisions and subdivisions. The encyclopedic arrangement makes it necessary to create an alphabetic list of all the captions in the subject file, including all the headings, divisions, and subdivisions in the file. Besides listing the headings, divisions, and subdivisions of the file, a good relative index will also list topics related to the actual captions in the file. For example, the captions listed below are taken from those actually used by the Colonial Williamsburg Foundation Archives and Records to file the wealth of information needed for the historic buildings on display. This is a small sampling of the encyclopedic arrangement used for the Peyton Randolph House. A similar listing would be used for the Brush-Everard House, Wythe House, Raleigh Tavern, and other buildings.

CAPTIONS	EXPLANATION
Peyton Randolph House	First heading
Architectural Details	First division of Peyton Randolph House
Chimney and Fireplaces	First division of Architectural Details
Doors and Windows	Second division of Architectural Details
Lanterns	Third division of Architectural Details
Lighting Fixtures	Fourth division of Architectural Details
Roofs and Gutters	Fifth division of Architectural Details
Venetian Blinds	Sixth division of Architectural Details
Wallpaper	Seventh division of Architectural Details
General	Miscellaneous folder placed after the alphabetic subject breakdowns
Building Materials	Second division of Peyton Randolph House
Brick	First division of Building Materials
Glass	Second division of Building Materials
Hardware	Third division of Building Materials
Lumber	Fourth division of Building Materials
Paint	Fifth division of Building Materials
Shingles	Sixth division of Building Materials
Stone	Seventh division of Building Materials
Tiles	Eighth division of Building Materials
General	Miscellaneous folder

A visitor to Colonial Williamsburg may wish to paint a room in the same color as one used in the living room of the Peyton Randolph House. The visitor could write Colonial Williamsburg for information about the color. The individual handling the request might first look in the relative index under *Paint*. Since this information is filed by the building, the relative index would have a cross-reference notation as shown below:

Paint   SEE   (Name of Building)

Suppose a file worker was trying to find information about the walls in the living room of the Peyton Randolph House. The cross-reference notation in the relative index might read:

Wall Coverings   SEE   Wallpaper
                              Paint

A relative index, then, can serve as a cross-reference for related topics as well as a direct reference to the captions in the subject file.

The most popular relative index used in the home is found in the back of any large cookbook. When deciding to make sugar cookies, for example, you would look under the major heading *Cookies* to find the particular recipe. Food, particularly, has fancy names, and the relative index helps you to find *Old-Fashioned Sugar Cookies.*

A subject file with *dictionary arrangement* has no divisions and subdivisions of subjects. Because the subjects are arranged in alphabetic sequence like the words in a dictionary, a relative index is not necessary. This type of alphabetic subject file is used in small businesses and other situations in which division of topics is not desired. One example of dictionary subject arrangement is the listing of types of businesses in the classified section, or yellow pages, of a telephone directory.

An alphabetic subject file with dictionary arrangement is shown at the bottom of this page.

Numeric Subject Files. Numeric subject filing uses code numbers for subject captions. Numeric subject filing has the advantages of any numeric filing system. Coding is much easier than with alphabetic subject systems because only a number, and not a long subject caption, is recorded on the record. The files are easier to expand because new topics can be placed at the end of the files rather than inserted in the middle, as with alphabetic files. Because all topics have a code number, they do not have to be arranged in alphabetic order. Therefore, another important advantage of numeric subject filing is that related topics can be placed conveniently near each

ALPHABETIC SUBJECT FILE WITH DICTIONARY ARRANGEMENT

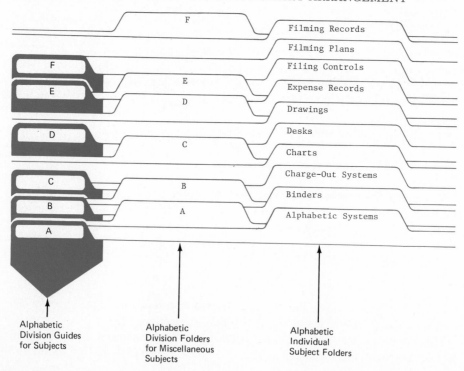

Alphabetic Division Guides for Subjects

Alphabetic Division Folders for Miscellaneous Subjects

Alphabetic Individual Subject Folders

other in the files without regard to alphabetic sequence. Of course, a card index is needed for numeric subject systems, just as it was needed for the numeric systems discussed in Chapter 6.

Three important types of numeric subject systems are simple-numeric, decimal-numeric, and duplex-numeric.

Simple-numeric subject systems usually have three-digit captions. The main headings are usually hundreds and are assigned first, as in this example of a system the Wholesale Grocery Suppliers might set up:

Breads	100	Fruits	500
Candies	200	Meats	600
Dairy Products	300	Spices & Dressings	700
Desserts	400	Vegetables	800

Then the divisions of each heading are assigned numbers that are hundreds and tens. For example:

Dairy Products	300
Butter	310
Cheese	320
Cream	330
Eggs	340
Milk	350

Finally, the subdivisions of each division are assigned numbers. Thus:

Milk	350
Buttermilk	351
Chocolate Milk	352
Skim Milk	353
Whole Milk	354

Notice that some numbers are not assigned, such as 900, 360, and 355. This allows for expansion in the event that new headings, divisions, or subdivisions are added later. The assigned numbers are placed on guides and folders in the file, sometimes together with the subject caption, sometimes alone.

A card is prepared for each heading, division, and subdivision in the file. The cards are arranged alphabetically to provide a reference for the code

ALPHABETIC INDEX CARD

Whole Milk   354

numbers assigned. The card for *Whole Milk* is shown on page 99 as an example. It would be filed under *W* in an alphabetic card index.

Decimal-numeric subject systems permit more subdivisions than simple-numeric systems. Up to the first subdivision, the decimal-numeric code numbers are the same as the simple-numeric codes, as:

Cream	330.
Sweet Cream	331.
Sour Cream	332.

The code 331. (Sweet Cream) can be further subdivided by adding one digit to the right of the decimal point, as:

Sweet Cream	331.
Heavy	331.1
Light	331.2

It is possible to continue the subdivisions by adding more digits to the right of a decimal point. The number 331.2 could be subdivided into 331.21, 331.22, 331.23, and so on.

Duplex-numeric subject systems, which use a number, a dash, and a second number, permit more than ten main headings and more than nine divisions under any one heading. (Simple-numeric and decimal-numeric systems are limited to ten main headings, 000–900, and nine main divisions under any one heading—110–190, for example.) Further subdivisions are possible with the duplex-numeric systems by adding a hyphen and beginning a new series of numbers. Some duplex-numeric systems use a combination of numbers and letters of the alphabet. The chart below shows how a main heading and its eleven divisions would be assigned codes in both simple-numeric and duplex-numeric systems. Note that the tenth and eleventh divisions cannot be coded in the simple-numeric system.

SUBJECT	SIMPLE-NUMERIC	DUPLEX-NUMERIC
Vegetables	800	8
Beans	810	8-1
Beets	820	8-2
Cabbage	830	8-3
Carrots	840	8-4
Lettuce	850	8-5
Peas	860	8-6
Potatoes	870	8-7
Radishes	880	8-8
Spinach	890	8-9
Squash	No provision	8-10
Turnips	No provision	8-11

The following table summarizes the numbering system for simple numeric, decimal-numeric, and duplex-numeric systems.

SIMPLE NUMERIC

500 Administration
  510 Meetings
    511 Staff Meetings
    512 Operations Meetings
    513 Review Meetings
    514 Technical Meetings

DECIMAL-NUMERIC

550. Administration
  551. Meetings
    551.1 Staff Meetings
    551.2 Operations Meetings
    551.3 Review Meetings
    551.4 Technical Meetings

DUPLEX-NUMERIC

5 Administration
  5-1 Meetings
    5-1-1 Staff Meetings
    5-1-2 Operations Meetings
    5-1-3 Review Meetings
    5-1-4 Technical Meetings

FILING PRACTICE

You are now ready to complete Jobs 37 to 40 of the *Practice Materials*.

STEPS IN SUBJECT CORRESPONDENCE FILING. You should follow these steps when you are filing papers according to subject.

Inspecting. As in alphabetic correspondence filing, the correspondence is checked for a release mark before filing.

Indexing and Coding. In alphabetic subject filing systems, it is usually necessary to write the subject classification in the upper right-hand corner of the correspondence. In numeric subject filing, the records are coded by writing the number in the upper right-hand corner as in numeric filing.

Because subject captions are not always apparent, the indexing of correspondence by subject is more difficult than indexing by individual or company name. Often the indexing step is performed by the executive who handles the correspondence. If the indexing is performed by a records specialist, the relative index is frequently consulted to determine the exact folder caption under which the correspondence is to be filed. If a piece of correspondence refers to more than one subject, a cross-reference sheet is prepared for the secondary subject.

Sorting. The coded records are sorted into piles using rough and fine sorting techniques as for other filing systems. In subject filing the first sort is done by the main heading. The successive sorts are done according to the subdivisions as many times as necessary.

Storing. The records for each folder are arranged chronologically with the most recent date on top. If the records are not dated, you might want to stamp them to indicate which is most recent. You may file alphabetically

STEPS IN THE SUBJECT FILING OF CORRESPONDENCE

1. INSPECTING. Correspondence is checked to make sure it has been released for filing.
2. INDEXING AND CODING. In an alphabetic-subject system it is usually necessary to write the subject classification in the upper right corner. (In a numeric-subject system, the records are coded by writing the folder number in the upper right corner.)
3. SORTING. The coded records are sorted into piles by main and then subheadings, whether they are alphabetic or numeric.

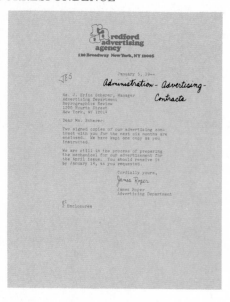

Next, these piles are sorted according to the divisions of the subheading.

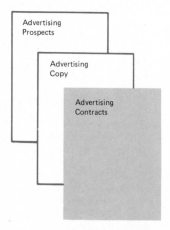

4. STORING. Records for each folder are arranged chronologically with the latest date in front and stored in file drawers.

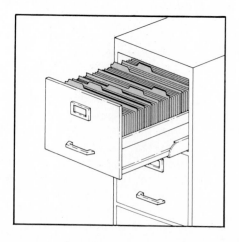

within each folder instead of by date depending on the subject. If the order of the contents is not a critical factor in the organization of the materials and their use, filing the most recent on top is the most efficient method to use. The steps in the subject filing of correspondence are shown on page 102.

Cross-Referencing.   When a piece of correspondence may be needed under more than one subject heading, a cross-reference sheet may be completed. Some businesses prefer to make a copy for the other locations. An example

CROSS-REFERENCING IN SUBJECT CORRESPONDENCE FILING

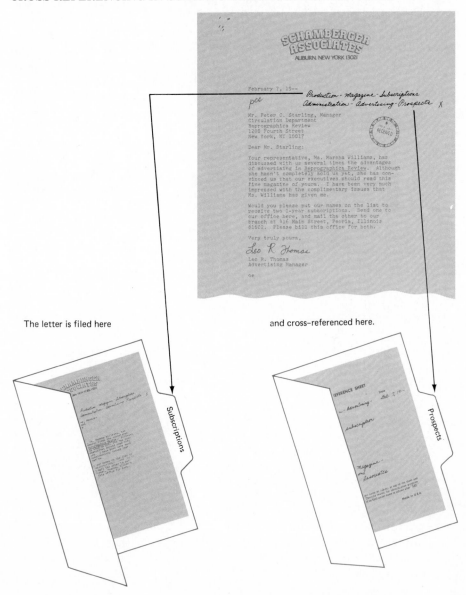

The letter is filed here

and cross-referenced here.

of a letter which may be filed by subject and cross-referenced is shown on page 103.

CHRONOLOGICAL FILING

A variation on subject filing is chronological filing; that is, filing items in order by date. This method is often used for follow-up of activities or information. You have already learned that correspondence can be filed chronologically with the most recent on top. Records can also be filed by date in sequence, grouped by day of the month, month, or year. Chapter 11 deals with chronological filing, which will help you with your day-to-day activities on the job.

━━━━━━━━━━ **FILING PRACTICE** ━━━━━━━━━━

You are now ready to complete Jobs 41 to 46 of the *Practice Materials*.

SURVEY OF COMPETENCIES

GENERAL REVIEW

You have had an opportunity to put into practice much of the material you have learned in this chapter. There are a few points, however, that you need to review to reinforce your competencies.

1. What is subject filing? (Competency 1)
2. Give two examples of the use of subject filing in business. (Competency 2)
3. List and describe the parts of a subject correspondence file. (Competency 3)
4. What are the steps in preparing correspondence to be filed by subject? (Competency 5)
5. How is cross-referencing done in subject systems? (Competency 5)
6. What are the three kinds of subject filing systems? (Competency 6)
7. What is chronological filing? (Competency 7)

CASE PROBLEMS

1. The Appliance Parts Supply Company operates a chain of stores selling parts for various appliances such as dishwashers, washers, and dryers. They use a subject filing system in which records of suppliers are filed according to the parts they manufacture. The purchasing department complains of difficulty in locating records when the name of a company, but not the product, is known. What can be done to eliminate this difficulty? (Competencies 2, 3)
2. You are a new employee working for the Durkin Pharmaceutical Company, which uses subject filing. You have difficulty locating rec-

ords you need to consult. You are hesitant to file any correspondence since you do not fully understand the system. How can you learn the system? (Competencies 2, 3, 5, 6)

3. The Tarantino Company uses a subject filing system. All the work in connection with filing, including the coding, has been performed in the filing department. The following proposal has been placed in the suggestion box for reducing confusion about the subject categories used for storing records: "Inasmuch as the department receiving an incoming letter is the one most likely to refer to it again after it has been stored, the coding should be done by that department rather than by the filing department." Do you think this suggestion should be adopted? Give your reasons. (Competencies 1, 2, 3, 5)

4. The office in which you work uses subject filing for miscellaneous information. At present there are eight drawers of assorted topics neatly arranged. The person who originated the system is no longer there; others in the office are as lost as you are when it comes to trying to locate something. Often you have had to look through two or three drawers to find what you need. You feel there has to be a better way. What is missing? What steps can you take to solve your problem with the files? (Competencies 2, 3)

5. A friend of yours, Janet Barnard, who works in a newly opened job placement office, would like to have some advice on setting up her files. She has decided that alphabetic filing will be unsuitable since she deals with job titles rather than individual names. She has eliminated numeric filing because she would like to group related information together for easy access. She has made a list of the folder captions she has started to set up. Later on she thinks she will need to divide the contents of some of these folders. What would you suggest? (Competencies 2, 3)

6. As part of your job for Richardson and Company, you need to keep some files pertaining to office equipment and employee activities. In addition, you are responsible for supplying information and forms to employees for various benefits and company needs. The person who had your job before you organized an alphabetic subject file with a dictionary arrangement. You feel another arrangement would be easier to work with. After reading the folder captions below and on the next page, make a list of the guides you will use and which folders will be placed behind each guide. Then make a relative index to go with your new file arrangement. Make any changes needed in these captions (explanations of contents are given in parentheses).

Annual Office Picnic
Bowling Team (social activity)
Business Cards (reorders)
Calculators (how to operate)
Calculators (repairs)
Christmas Party

Company Policy and Procedures Handouts
Copiers (operating instructions)
Copiers—Repairs
Duplicating Equipment (operating instructions)
Employee Health Insurance Coverage Change Forms
Employee Health Insurance Claim Forms
Employee Health Insurance Information
Employee Life Insurance Applications and Claim Forms
Employee Life Insurance Information
Employee Training Program: Work and Time Managment Seminar
Equipment Operating Instructions: Typing Equipment
Forms (ordering information)
Human Relations Seminar (for employees)
Income Tax Withholding Forms
Letterhead and Other Stationery Supplies
Personnel Information Blanks (to update personnel files)
Repairs on Duplicating Equipment
Office Supplies (small items)
Typing Equipment Repairs
WP/DP Integration Seminar (for employees)
(Competency 8)

7. Now that you have reorganized your file in Case Problem 6, you are ready to file the following items which are in your "To Be Filed" basket (indicate captions of new folders as necessary):

   a. A suggestion from Andy Cummings for a restaurant to consider when selecting a place for next year's Christmas party
   b. A request from Mr. Jones, your boss, to order more business cards for him the next time you place an order
   c. Information concerning a workshop that many employees attended on the new telephone system being installed
   d. A new supply of health insurance claim forms
   e. An invoice which has been paid for repairs on one of the calculating machines (the invoices are kept as records of the repair)
   f. A request from Sandy Smith to order some paper clips, pens, and note pads when you place your next order
   g. A program from the Human Relations Seminar that Dan Evans borrowed and returned to you today
   h. A note about a minor problem with the duplicating machine which can be fixed the next time you have to call in someone to repair something more important
   i. A note attached to an advertising brochure to consider a new supplier for letterhead the next time you place an order.
   (Competency 9)

If you have not mastered all of the competencies reviewed in the Survey, reread that part of the chapter which deals with the competency in question; then recheck your progress.

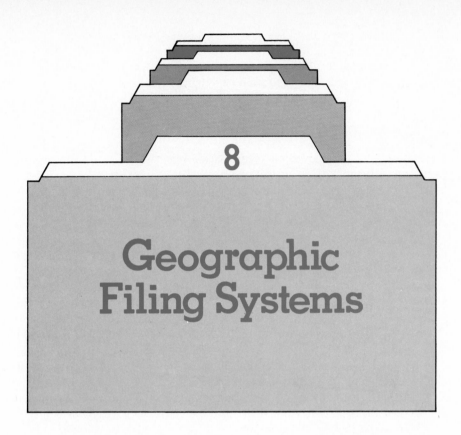

Geographic Filing Systems

When you have completed this chapter, you will be able to:

1. Define geographic filing.
2. Give examples of business situations in which geographic filing is used.
3. List and describe the parts of the geographic correspondence file.
4. File and find cards using a geographic filing system. (See Jobs 47 to 50 in the *Practice Materials*.)
5. List and describe the steps in geographic correspondence filing.
6. Index and code correspondence for filing, prepare cross-references, and file and find correspondence using a geographic filing system. (See Jobs 51 to 55 in the *Practice Materials*.)
7. Select guide and folder captions when given a list of items which are to be filed using a geographic system.
8. Assign various items to the proper caption when given a list of geographic captions. (See Jobs 47 to 55 in the *Practice Materials*.)

DEFINITION OF GEOGRAPHIC FILING

Geographic filing is an alphabetic arrangement of records first according to location and then according to name or subject.

WHEN GEOGRAPHIC FILING IS USED

Geographic filing is used when records filed by location serve the organization more efficiently than if they were filed in any other way.

Sales organizations, for example, may classify customers by territories or states to provide a mailing list that will speed the sorting of outgoing mail as required by the U.S. Postal Service. Public utilities, which have thousands of customers, may divide the areas they serve into geographic districts with a branch office in each district. National service organizations, such as the Boy Scouts and Girl Scouts, are organized geographically by state and by division or council within the state; other organizations may be set up by region, state, city, town, village, county, or township. Real estate firms use listings organized by names of the sections of the city such as *Glendale, North Park, Northhampton, Oakwood Terrace, Ranch Estates,* and *Riverdale.*

The telephone book is an example of geographic filing with listings in alphabetic order for the white pages and in alphabetic subject order in the yellow pages. In some areas of the country one or more towns will compose a regional area; in others each town may be listed separately in the telephone book, with two or more adjoining towns included in the same book. Usually the division depends on whether or not the numbers can be dialed without charge to the calling party.

GEOGRAPHIC CARD FILES

For some situations, a card file of information organized by location is useful. For example, a salesperson might keep a card file of all customers in a specific area to notify when a visit is being planned. A utility company might keep a card file of customers arranged by street name. Charitable organizations frequently organize pledge cards and other records by territory to help divide the work load so that a personal follow-up may be made with greatest efficiency.

Card files are also necessary to serve as a card index to the main geographic correspondence files.

GEOGRAPHIC CORRESPONDENCE FILES

As has been stated, geographic filing is used when records need to be grouped by location rather than name.

A GEOGRAPHIC CROSS-REFERENCE CARD

```
Tenn., Bristol, Rogers Construction Co.

SEE:  Tenn., Memphis, Rogers Construction Co.
```

ORGANIZATION OF GEOGRAPHIC CORRESPONDENCE FILES.   There are two main parts to the geographic correspondence filing system: the main geographic files and the card index. A real estate company, for example, would group leases and the correspondence about its rental properties in a main geographic file; an alphabetic correspondence file by name of tenant would be inefficient since the tenants change. A card index arranged alphabetically according to the name of the tenant, however, is necessary to save time when the address is not known. For those records which do not fit the geographic system, alphabetic or subject files may be set up.

ARRANGEMENT OF RECORDS IN FOLDERS.   Within the individual folders in a geographic file, records are arranged chronologically, with the record bearing the latest date in front. In the town or city miscellaneous folders, records are arranged alphabetically first by the names of the correspondents and then chronologically for each correspondent. In the state miscellaneous folders, records are arranged first alphabetically by the name of the town or city, then alphabetically by the name of the correspondent, and finally chronologically for each correspondent. The three steps that a record might undergo in a geographic file, beginning with the state miscellaneous folder, are illustrated on page 110.

STEPS IN GEOGRAPHIC CORRESPONDENCE FILING.   The steps in geographic correspondence filing are similar to those in subject correspondence filing. The illustration on page 111 outlines the process in detail.

Inspecting.   Correspondence is checked to make sure it has been released for filing.

Indexing and Coding.   The name of the correspondent and the location under which the record is to be filed are determined. The location may be

MISCELLANEOUS AND INDIVIDUAL FOLDERS IN A GEO-GRAPHIC CORRESPONDENCE FILE

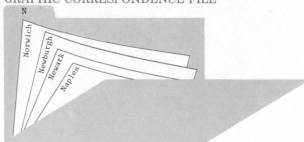

1. Records pertaining to towns within a state are stored in the state miscellaneous folders. The miscellaneous folder at the left is for towns in New York with names that begin with *N*.

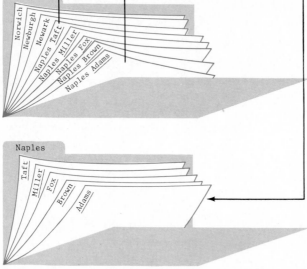

2. When enough records pertaining to one town or city have accumulated in the state miscellaneous folder, a town or city miscellaneous folder is opened for that town or city.

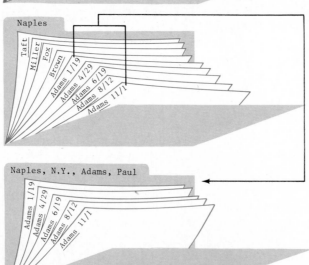

3. When enough records have accumulated in the town or city miscellaneous folder pertaining to one correspondent, an individual folder is opened for that correspondent.

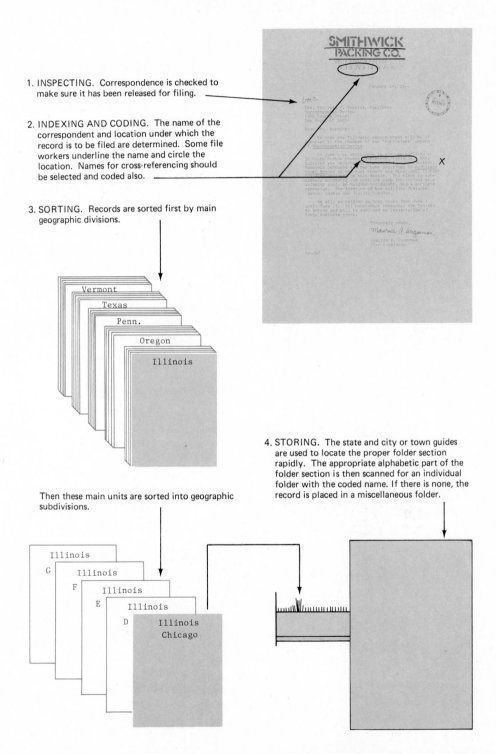

1. INSPECTING. Correspondence is checked to make sure it has been released for filing.

2. INDEXING AND CODING. The name of the correspondent and location under which the record is to be filed are determined. Some file workers underline the name and circle the location. Names for cross-referencing should be selected and coded also.

3. SORTING. Records are sorted first by main geographic divisions.

Then these main units are sorted into geographic subdivisions.

4. STORING. The state and city or town guides are used to locate the proper folder section rapidly. The appropriate alphabetic part of the folder section is then scanned for an individual folder with the coded name. If there is none, the record is placed in a miscellaneous folder.

circled to make it more distinctive since the name of the organization is also underlined. If cross-referencing under a second location is necessary, it should be done at this time.

Sorting.   Records are sorted first by the main geographic divisions and then by the subdivisions.

Storing.   The guides of the geographic divisions and subdivisions are used to locate the individual folder. If there is no individual folder, the record is placed in the miscellaneous folder for that division or subdivision. A miscellaneous folder for a state, for example, will hold correspondence for all cities and towns in the state that have less than five pieces of correspondence. This avoids overloading the files with town or city folders with few papers in them. When five or more records have accumulated for one correspondent in a miscellaneous folder, an individual folder is opened up as shown in the illustration on page 110.

A GEOGRAPHIC CROSS-REFERENCE SHEET

CROSS-REFERENCE SHEET

Name or Subject   Date
    Illinois, Maplewood   Jan. 19, 19--
    Smithwick Packing Co.

Regarding
    News Release

SEE
Name or Subject

    Illinois, Chicago
    Smithwick Packing Co.

File cross-reference sheet under name or subject at top of the sheet and by the latest date of papers. Describe matter for identification purposes. The papers, themselves, should be filed under name or subject after "SEE."

Made in U.S.A.

GEOGRAPHIC FILE DRAWER ARRANGEMENT

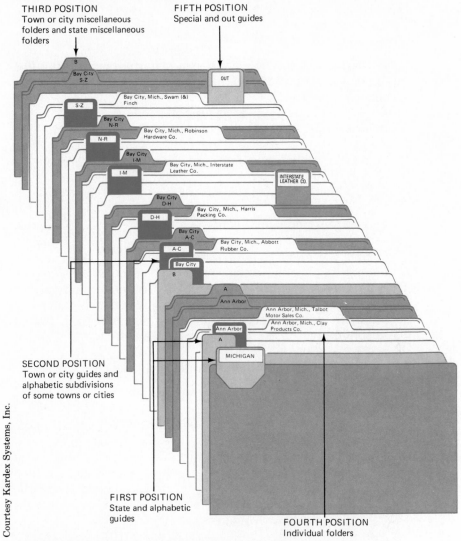

THIRD POSITION
Town or city miscellaneous
folders and state miscellaneous
folders

FIFTH POSITION
Special and out guides

SECOND POSITION
Town or city guides and
alphabetic subdivisions
of some towns or cities

FIRST POSITION
State and alphabetic
guides

FOURTH POSITION
Individual folders

Courtesy Kardex Systems, Inc.

A geographic file has guide and folder tabs arranged from left to right.
Notice that five city miscellaneous folders, subdivided by alphabetic
range, and five individual folders prevent overcrowding of records for
Bay City.

Cross-Referencing. The cross-referencing of records in the geographic correspondence filing system is shown on page 112. The coding may be done
on the correspondence and copies or cross-reference sheets prepared for the
other folder(s). In some cases the cross-referencing may be done in the card
index.

TYPICAL GEOGRAPHIC FILES. Let us see how the contents of a typical file
drawer, such as the one that is illustrated above, are arranged (1) looking

from front to back and (2) looking at the position of the tabs from left to right.

1. Looking from front to back:

   a. In the front is a guide covering a major segment of the file. This is called a *state guide,* and its tab has the caption *Michigan.*

   b. Behind the state guide is an *alphabetic guide,* and its tab has the caption *A.* It covers all cities in Michigan beginning with *A.*

   c. Behind the alphabetic guide is a *town or city guide* for the town of *Ann Arbor.*

   d. Behind the town guide are *individual folders* for correspondents in Ann Arbor.

   e. Behind the individual folders is a *town or city miscellaneous folder,* and its tab has the caption *Ann Arbor* for correspondents in Ann Arbor who do not warrant an individual folder.

   f. Behind the town miscellaneous folder is a *state miscellaneous folder* with the caption *A* for towns in Michigan beginning with *A* that do not warrant a town or city miscellaneous folder. For example, correspondence pertaining to Alma, Michigan, would be stored in the *A* state miscellaneous folder.

2. Looking at the position of the tabs from left to right:

   First position: *State guides* and *alphabetic guides*
   Second position: *Town or city guides*
   Third position: *Town or city miscellaneous folders* and *state miscellaneous folders*
   Fourth position: *Individual folders* (The caption gives the name of the town or city first, the state second, and then the correspondent. The town is listed before the state because the town guide is nearby, making cross-checking easy.)
   Fifth position: *Special guides* and *out guides*

Sometimes, when there is a large volume of correspondence for one town or city, the correspondence in a town or city miscellaneous folder is alphabetically subdivided. In the illustration, for example, *Bay City* has been subdivided so that there are five miscellaneous folders for Bay City, each for a different alphabetic group. There is a guide for each of the subdivided folders.

━━━━━━━━━━━ FILING PRACTICE ━━━━━━━━━━━

You are now ready to complete Jobs 47 to 55 of the *Practice Materials.*

SURVEY OF COMPETENCIES

GENERAL REVIEW

You have had an opportunity to put into practice much of the material you have learned in this chapter. There are a few points, however, that you need to review to reinforce your competencies.

1. What is geographic filing? (Competency 1)
2. Give examples of two business situations in which geographic filing is used. (Competency 2)
3. List and describe the parts of the geographic correspondence file. (Competency 3)
4. What are the steps in preparing correspondence to be filed in a geographic system? (Competency 5)
5. How is cross-referencing done in geographic filing systems? (Competency 6)

CASE PROBLEMS

1. The Moore Equipment Company operates within the boundaries of California. Ninety percent of its business is conducted in the cities of Los Angeles, San Diego, and San Francisco. The remainder is done in the twenty-five cities and towns listed below. What primary and secondary guide captions should the company decide upon when it sets up its geographic filing system? (Competency 7)

   a. Anaheim
   b. Bakersfield
   c. Burbank
   d. Fresno
   e. Glendale
   f. Lompoc
   g. Newport Beach
   h. Oakland
   i. Oceanside
   j. Oxnard
   k. Palm Springs
   l. Pasadena
   m. Redwood City
   n. Riverside
   o. Sacramento
   p. Salinas
   q. San Bernadino
   r. San Jose
   s. San Mateo
   t. Santa Ana
   u. Santa Barbara
   v. Santa Cruz
   w. Santa Monica
   x. Sunnyvale
   y. Ventura

2. The Patio Equipment Company now has two types of miscellaneous folders in its geographic file: (a) town or city and (b) state. One of the file workers, Nancy Jorgenson, has suggested that the state miscellaneous folders be eliminated. If you were her file supervisor would you follow Nancy's suggestion? (Competency 3)

3. Your employer supervises eight salespersons who work the territories in your state. Records are stored geographically by city. Andrew Constable, Shirley McIntosh, and Darlene Sparkman have been hired

recently to fill three vacancies on the sales staff. You find that they are having difficulty locating some of the folders they need since they are unfamiliar with the area and do not know which customers are in which cities. Some customers have branches in more than one city. How can you help these three individuals? (Competency 3)

If you have not mastered all of the competencies reviewed in the Survey, reread that part of the chapter which deals with the competency in question; then recheck your progress.

9

Records Control and Retention

When you have completed this chapter, you will be able to:

1. Define the terms *charge system, records control, records inventory, records retention, retention period,* and *tickler file.*
2. List and describe the parts of a charge system.
3. Name three substitutes for a folder or record in the files.
4. List steps to take when locating a lost record or folder.
5. State at least four questions that should be considered when deciding whether or not records should be transferred.
6. Name three plans for the transfer of records and describe how each plan works.
7. List the steps in the transfer process.
8. Describe how records can be obtained for use from storage.
9. List four methods for disposing of records.

RECORDS CONTROL

Records control refers to the procedures used to keep track of records after they have been created or received and stored in the files. When a business does not have established procedures for using the material in the files, records may be lost, kept for individual use, or never used, once stored. Employees cannot do their jobs efficiently if records are not available or if they are so hard to get that it is easier to do without them. Without proper procedures, the business runs the risk of losing valuable time and money attempting to find needed records.

The path of a letter after it is received was outlined on page 59. Incoming mail is date- and time-stamped to verify receipt. Correspondence created in the office is ready for filing along with incoming correspondence which has been used when it is placed in a special folder or out basket for "To Be Filed" materials. Large organizations employ individuals whose job it is to see that materials are filed promptly and their use controlled. Control of the files is accomplished by means of a charge system.

CHARGE SYSTEMS

A charge system assures that all records are accounted for whether they are in the files or in use. The complexity of the system will be determined by the needs of the business. A sales firm, for example, would use a system that makes it possible to locate quickly any information needed on customers. A government installation would need a system that restricts the use of secret information to a designated area. Only those individuals with a "need to know" would be allowed access. When not in use, the records would be locked in special filing cabinets called *safes* under the supervision and responsibility of a designated individual.

PARTS OF A CHARGE SYSTEM. A charge system usually consists of the following parts:

1. A requisition form to be completed by the individual making the request for the record or file folder.
2. A replacement record for the record removed, usually an out card or substitution sheet.
3. A follow-up system to assure that the materials are returned to the files.
4. A method for obtaining materials which have not been returned and for locating materials which have become lost.

Requisition. In a large office records may be requested by telephone, by interoffice mail, by messenger, or in person. A requisition form should be completed either by the person making the request or by a file worker. The requisition form should include the information listed in the illustration on page 119.

Whenever possible the requisition form should be signed by the borrower to establish responsibility for the whereabouts of the record. It is also a good idea to have the borrower's office number or department on the form.

In a small office where requests are made personally and where the borrower removes the records from the files, the use of a requisition form

REQUISITION FORM

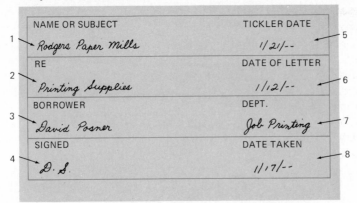

NAME OR SUBJECT	TICKLER DATE
Rodgers Paper Mills	1/21/--
RE	DATE OF LETTER
Printing Supplies	1/12/--
BORROWER	DEPT.
David Posner	Job Printing
SIGNED	DATE TAKEN
D. S.	1/17/--

The following information is given on the requisition:
(1) the name indexed on the borrowed record, (2) what
the record is about or pertains to, (3) the name of the
borrower, (4) the name of the person who obtained the
record, (5) the date the record is to be returned, (6) the
date of the record, (7) the borrower's department, and
(8) the date the record was borrowed.

will not be necessary if the items are returned to the files immediately.
Instead of following formal procedures, the borrower should give a note to
the person responsible for the files stating where the record is, so that if
anyone else needs the record, there will be no problem locating it.

Replacement Record.   When an entire folder is removed from the files, a
replacement record, such as an *out folder* or an *out guide,* should be placed
in the location of the borrowed folder. When an individual paper is removed
from a folder, a *substitution card* should be placed in the folder exactly
where the paper was. These replacement records indicate who has the
record and the date it was removed from the files. They are useful in three
ways: (1) they show that records are being used and have not been lost or
misfiled, (2) they enable the file worker to follow up the borrowed records
to make sure they get back to the file, and (3) they act as bookmarks to
make refiling easy.

Out guides are made of the same heavy cardboard as file guides. Two
popular types that may be obtained are (1) a guide with a pocket at the
front for a requisition slip or (2) a cumulative guide on which information
on the missing record is written. Both kinds of out guides have advantages:
the pocket type eliminates the need for transferring the information on the
requisition slip; the cumulative type provides a history of how the records
have been used and by whom.

Cumulative guides are usually printed on both sides and are simply
turned over when one side is full. These guides are handy in small offices
where the employees know each other and can easily obtain a file directly
from the user indicated on the guide. Some offices prefer to use out folders
instead of out guides. With an out folder, new records that need to be stored

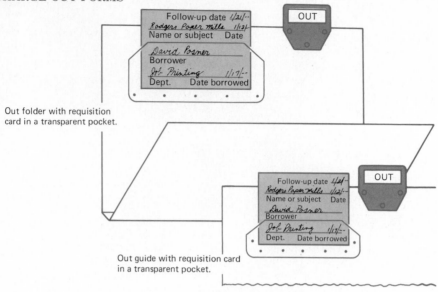

Out folder with requisition
card in a transparent pocket.

Out guide with requisition card
in a transparent pocket.

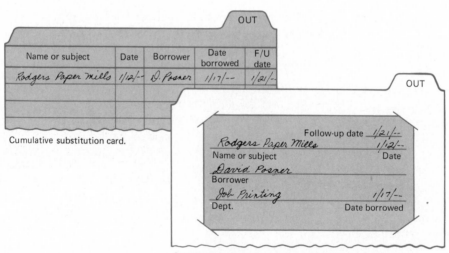

Cumulative substitution card.

Substitution card with requisition card attached.

Even though these charge-out forms differ in size and makeup, each one
contains (1) the name indexed on the borrowed record, (2) the date of
the record, (3) the name of the borrower, (4) the date the record was
borrowed, and (5) the date the record is to be returned (follow-up date).

in the file may be stored temporarily and transferred to the permanent file
folder when it is returned. The front of an out folder may be like a guide
with a pocket or like a cumulative guide.

Another method of providing a replacement record is to keep the original
folder in the drawer and transfer the contents to a special *carrier folder*.

Carrier folders are made of a heavy material that can withstand extensive handling. Furthermore, they are usually of a distinctive color, which signals their importance. This helps prevent their loss and expedites their return to the files.

As with out guides, substitution cards may be either the pocket type or the cumulative type. These cards are of a special color and are small enough to be inserted in a folder to indicate the absence of a paper.

Some records which are requested may need to be used by more than one individual. There are two ways to accomplish this transfer efficiently:

1. A routing slip may be attached to the records that are requested and a copy of the routing slip kept with the charge out form. The routing slip will list the names of all the individuals who will be using the records. After use, the user places a check mark on the form. This indicates that the records are ready to be passed on to the next person.

ROUTING SLIP

ROUTING SLIP

Date _____

To:		Signed	Date
1.	General Manager		
2.	Business Manager		
3.	Marketing Director		
4.			
5.			

From: _____

Purpose/Comments:

Some routing slips have information printed on them to save time in routing.

2. A recharge form may be filled out and forwarded to the file department. This user change is then indicated on the replacement record and the out card in the file.

Follow-Up System. The length of time records may be allowed out of the file is determined by the needs of the borrowers, the value of the records,

FOLLOW-UP NOTICE

To ___David Posner___   Date ___1/21/--___

From ___Central Files___

Our records indicate that you have not yet returned the following material:

Rodgers Paper Mills--letter of 1/12/--.

Please return by ___1/28/--___
or complete the attached recharge form.

A follow-up notice reminds the borrower that a record is due and may tell the borrower that an extension of time to return it will be allowed.

RECHARGE FORM

RECHARGE FORM

Date ___1/28/--___

Name ___David Posner___   Dept. ___Job Printing___

Name of person
to whom records
are charged out ___David Posner___

Record ___Rodgers Paper Mills, letter, 1/12/--___

Due Date (old) ___1/21/--___

Date records will be returned ___2/4/--___

The recharge form allows a borrower to establish a new due date. The borrower may be the same person who originally borrowed the record or another person.

and the need for security. In any event, a time limit should be established for use of borrowed records. If they are to be kept longer than the time allowed, the records should be recharged to the user. It is important to note that the longer records remain out of the files, the greater the chances for losing or misplacing the records.

When a record is requested, a duplicate copy of the requisition form may be placed in a follow-up file, called a *tickler file,* under the due date. When the record is returned, the requisition form is pulled and destroyed. A form for records requested in advance of the date needed may also be included in the tickler file. On the date the record is needed, a notation should be made that the record was released and the date it should be returned.

The file worker checks the tickler file daily to see if there are any records which have not yet been returned. After checking the file cabinet to make

TICKLER FILE FOR FOLLOWING UP ON BORROWED RECORDS

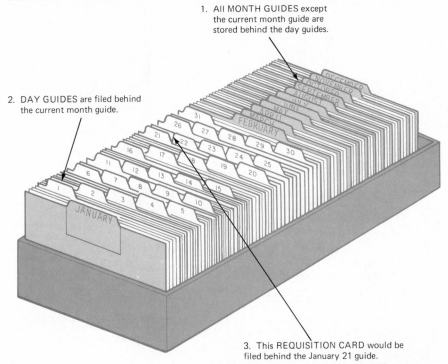

1. All MONTH GUIDES except the current month guide are stored behind the day guides.

2. DAY GUIDES are filed behind the current month guide.

3. This REQUISITION CARD would be filed behind the January 21 guide.

NAME OR SUBJECT	TICKLER DATE
Rodgers Paper Mills	1/21/--
RE	DATE OF LETTER
Printing Supplies	1/12/--
BORROWER	DEPT.
David Posner	Job Printing
SIGNED	DATE TAKEN
D. S.	1/17/--

certain that the records have not been returned, the file worker sends a notice to the borrower requesting the prompt return of the records or the completion of a recharge form.

System for Locating a Lost Record.   Refer to the illustration below for an orderly procedure for searching for a lost record. In addition to the eight

HOW TO CONDUCT AN ORGANIZED SEARCH FOR A LOST RECORD

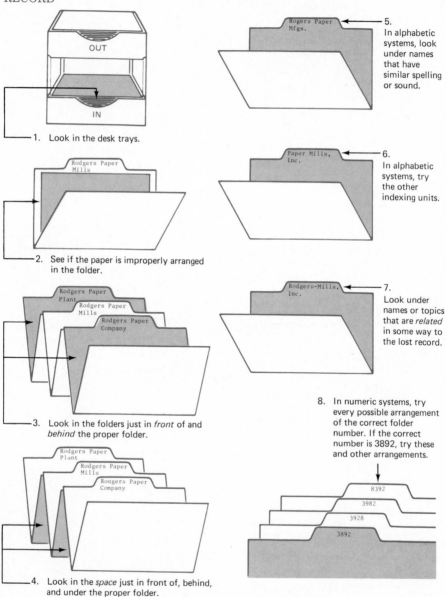

1. Look in the desk trays.

2. See if the paper is improperly arranged in the folder.

3. Look in the folders just in *front* of and *behind* the proper folder.

4. Look in the *space* just in front of, behind, and under the proper folder.

5. In alphabetic systems, look under names that have similar spelling or sound.

6. In alphabetic systems, try the other indexing units.

7. Look under names or topics that are *related* in some way to the lost record.

8. In numeric systems, try every possible arrangement of the correct folder number. If the correct number is 3892, try these and other arrangements.

steps given in the illustration, you might check wastebaskets, ask individuals who borrowed the record in the recent past, and see whether the record has been transferred to a transfer location outside the main storage area. If you cannot locate the record, then construct as best you can from memory the contents of the record and place that information in the folder.

Similar steps to those suggested for a lost record may be used when attempting to locate a lost folder. Ask individuals in the office to be on the lookout for the file. Be cautious that you do not accuse individuals of taking and losing the file. If you approach this problem with a cooperative attitude, others will be willing to help you.

A secretary or other office worker who is responsible for files that may be consulted by other employees should establish a system for keeping files in order so that records are not lost. A log for borrowers to enter a short description of the record removed with space for the date when borrowed and initials of borrower and date returned would serve the purpose. Another system might be to set up an out box and an in box on top of the file cabinet. A borrower would drop a slip indicating the record borrowed and the date and initials of the borrower into the out box, and would place the returned record in the in box.

TRANSFER AND DISPOSAL

Transfer involves making decisions about what records to retain and what records to destroy. Of the records that are retained, decisions must then be made about where to keep them: in present storage locations suitable for frequent use, or in transfer storage locations that are out of the way but suitable for the infrequent occasions when they might be needed. Regular transfer of records is necessary to conserve space, equipment, and labor. The alternative is overcrowded file drawers, time lost in retrieving records, and crowding of office space with file cabinets. Records that are transferred should be reviewed periodically to determine which may be destroyed, so that space will be cleared for newly transferred records. Whether or not records should be transferred depends on answers to the following questions:

1. How valuable are the records? (Are they worth the cost of keeping them?)
2. How often do they need to be used?
3. Where can the records be stored?
4. Is the retention of the records necessary for legal purposes?
5. What company requirements exist for the retention of these records?
6. Should the records be destroyed? If yes, when? If no, what special precautions need to be taken to ensure they will not be lost or destroyed accidentally?

RECORD TITLE Customer Ledgers

INVENTORY			RETENTION		
DEPARTMENT Accounting			APPROVALS		YEARS
RECORD COPY [X] DUPLICATE COPY [ ]			RECOMMENDED (SPECIFY SOURCE) Company policy		5
VOLUME			ADMINISTRATIVE BY *Henrietta Smythe* DATE 3/1/80		
INCLUSIVE DATES	LOCATION	QUANTITY	LEGAL COUNSEL BY *Andrew Watson* DATE 3/2/80		
3/16/80–3/31/80	OFFICE	25	EXECUTIVE BY *Patricia Vazonna* DATE 3/5/80		
	STORAGE				
REMARKS Ledgers 1000–1025			FINALIZED SCHEDULE		
			IN OFFICE 1/25/81	IN STORAGE 1/27/81	DESTROY
			BY DATE		
			SPECIAL INSTRUCTIONS		
COUNTED BY		DATE 1/20/81			

FORM 1606   RECORDS INVENTORY AND RETENTION CONTROL CARD   **BB** BANKERS BOX
                                                                                   records storage systems

Courtesy Bankers Box

Customer ledgers for 3/16/80 to 3/31/80 are counted and recorded on the inventory side of this form. On the retention side, authorization to retain them for five years is given, with authorized signatures. Anyone needing the customer ledgers on 1/25/81 would obtain them from the office; two days later they would be available from the transfer storage location.

RECORDS RETENTION. *Records retention* is the decision to keep records depending on their usefulness, legal requirements, and other factors which may be determined by the business or organization. The length of time that these records must or will be kept in active, inactive, or transfer files before they are destroyed is the *retention period.*

Whether a business keeps or destroys some records is not always a matter of choice. Various requirements for keeping records are mandated by federal, state, and local governments. The business itself has a need to keep many records for specified periods of time because past experience is needed as an aid in making current business decisions. There may be historical or archival reasons for keeping other records. An organization such as Colonial Williamsburg Foundation spends large sums of money on research for building restoration and study of archaeological diggings. These findings are filed for historical purposes.

When the records retention schedule for a business is being planned, an authority on the subject should be consulted to examine the kinds of records the business has and what legal requirements exist for these records.

New laws on social issues such as equal employment and proper use of the environment have forced business firms to think about the possible social consequences of their operations. Business firms need to keep records that may serve as evidence of their respect for and obedience to these laws.

Records that are classified as *vital* should not be destroyed. These records are usually retained in a vault or a safe for protection from fire, theft, and other disasters. Examples of vital records are:

Corporate charter

Correspondence containing information that may be needed for legal reasons

Deeds, mortgage, and bills of sale or contracts for major business transactions

Minute books of meetings of boards of directors and stockholders

Stocks and bonds

Tax returns

Trademark registrations

Records that are classified as *important* may be kept for about six to seven years. Examples of these records are:

Accounts receivable ledgers

Accounts payable ledgers

Canceled checks

Creditor invoices

Customer invoices

Inventory records

Payroll records

Purchase orders

Time books

Records classified as *useful* may be kept for perhaps one to three years. Examples of these records are:

Bank reconciliations

Employment applications

General correspondence

Insurance policies that have expired

Petty cash vouchers

Receiving records

Stenographers' notebooks

Printed schedules that list the kinds of business records that should be retained and the length of time to retain them are available from equipment manufacturers. However, every business must make adaptations for its own needs and set up its own schedule. File workers often make decisions on what papers to retain and what papers to destroy, and common sense will dictate the proper decision. Obviously, papers that deal with routine events that have already taken place may be destroyed (reminders of meetings, out-of-date pamphlets, letters requesting information on a product, and so on). Papers that may be needed for future reference, such as those dealing with financial matters, should be retained.

MERGING FILES. In the process of making decisions about transfer of records, you might find it efficient to merge certain files. You may combine the contents of two or more folders into one, either using the caption of one of the old folders or creating a new caption to cover the new combination of contents. You may have had files for *Typewriter Repairs, Duplicating Machine Repairs,* and *Calculating Machine Repairs.* You could merge the contents of these folders into one with the caption *Office Machines Repairs.* Suppose you had done business with Jones Company over a period of years. During that time, you had set up several files for their records. Some of the correspondence contained in these files is routine and of no value after a few months; other records may need to be kept for several years. By eliminating the routine correspondence, you may be able to combine the records of two or more folders into one.

PLANS OF TRANSFER. There are several plans for the transfer of records. The one selected will depend on the nature and frequency of reference, the space available, and the filing system in use. In general, transfer plans are either *periodic* or *perpetual.*

Periodic. Periodic transfer is the removal of papers at the end of a definite *filing period* (at the end of each year, for example) from the active files to inexpensive transfer files. Periodic transfer can be operated in at least three ways: one period, two period, or maximum-minimum period.

In the one-period plan, only the papers for the current filing period occupy the active files. On certain dates the folders and their contents are moved directly to the transfer files and a new filing period is started. Even though this transfer plan is easy to operate, it has a definite disadvantage. For a while, frequent trips will have to be made to the transfer files to consult records from the previous filing period. If the transfer files are located away from the office, much valuable time may be lost.

In the two-period plan, the files are divided to provide space for two filing periods—the present period and the period immediately preceding. Records of the present period are referred to as *active;* those of the previous period are called *inactive.* At the end of each filing period, the following changes take place: (1) the inactive records are removed to transfer files, (2) the active records become inactive and are placed in the inactive drawers, and (3) the active drawers are now empty, ready to receive records for the next filing period. This plan eliminates the disadvantage of the one-period plan because only the oldest papers have been removed to transfer files, and the current records and the records of the previous period are still readily

A-B ACTIVE	M-N ACTIVE
C-E ACTIVE	O-R ACTIVE
F-H ACTIVE	S-T ACTIVE
I-L ACTIVE	U-Z ACTIVE

With the one-period plan, all file drawers are active.

With the two-period plan and five-drawer files, inactive files often may be contracted to fit the top and the bottom drawers.

A-E INACTIVE	I-Q INACTIVE
A-B ACTIVE	M-N ACTIVE
C-F ACTIVE	O-S ACTIVE
G-L ACTIVE	T-Z ACTIVE
F-H INACTIVE	R-Z INACTIVE

A-E ACTIVE	L-R ACTIVE
F-K ACTIVE	S-Z ACTIVE
A-E INACTIVE	L-R INACTIVE
F-K INACTIVE	S-Z INACTIVE

With the two-period plan and four-drawer files, the upper two rows hold active papers, and the lower two rows hold inactive records.

In this two-period plan, the active files stand beside the inactive.

A-B ACTIVE	A-B INACTIVE	K-L ACTIVE	K-L INACTIVE
C ACTIVE	C INACTIVE	M-N ACTIVE	M-N INACTIVE
D-E ACTIVE	D-E INACTIVE	O-R ACTIVE	O-R INACTIVE
F-G ACTIVE	F-G INACTIVE	S ACTIVE	S INACTIVE
H-J ACTIVE	H-J INACTIVE	T-Z ACTIVE	T-Z INACTIVE

available. With a two-period plan, the fatigue that comes from working in a stooped or tip-toe position can be reduced by reserving easily accessible file drawers for active records.

An adaptation of the two-period plan to eliminate switching records from active to inactive file drawers at the end of a filing period operates as follows: An active cabinet stands beside an inactive one. At the end of a filing period, the records in the active cabinet automatically become inactive, and they are not moved. The records in the inactive cabinet are transferred, leaving this cabinet empty—ready for new records. Then, simply by interchanging "active" and "inactive" drawer labels, the file worker readies the two cabinets for the next period.

In the maximum-minimum period plan, the least recent papers are moved directly from the active files to the transfer files at the end of each filing period. Inactive files are not used. However, because the most recent records are kept in the active files, the disadvantage of the one-period plan is

Records Control and Retention 129

overcome. To use this plan, a business must establish maximum and minimum periods of time for keeping records in the active files.

A business may want papers up to 6 months old in the files. At specified intervals, every 3 months, for example, the folders would be checked for papers which are older than 6 months which should be transferred to storage files. The records removed would be between 6 and 9 months old. In another 3 months the process would be repeated. Suppose the business received a letter dated January 9. The transfer dates used by this business are January 1, April 1, July 1, and October 1. The January 9 letter would remain in the files during the April 1 transfer and during the July 1 transfer because on that date it would not yet be 6 months old. It would be transferred on October 1. An advantage of this system is that it keeps current papers in the files. A disadvantage is that each folder must be checked, a time-consuming process.

HOW THE MAXIMUM-MINIMUM TRANSFER PLAN OPERATES

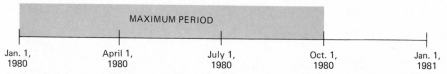

1. On October 1, 1980, files contain records from as early as January 1, 1980, or nine months old (maximum period).

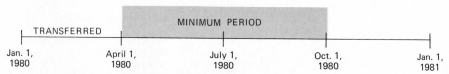

2. On the same day, October 1, 1980, records of the earliest three months are transferred, leaving records of the last six months (minimum period).

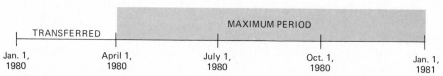

3. Three months later, January 1, 1981, the files have accumulated the records of the past nine months (maximum period).

4. On the same day, January 1, 1981, records of the earliest three months are transferred again, leaving records of the last six months (minimum period).

Perpetual. Under the perpetual plan, papers are transferred from the active files constantly, or *perpetually.* This plan is generally used when the nature of a business makes it difficult to set definite filing periods. For example, in the type of work done by building contractors, architects, or lawyers, the length of time taken to complete the work varies with each job or case. Transferring records on a periodic basis might result, therefore, in the removal of frequently used records. Under the perpetual transfer plan, whenever a job or case is completed, all records pertaining to it are moved from the active files to the inactive or transfer files. This transfer of completed work is the biggest advantage of the perpetual transfer system since on any given day only records in current use are in the active files.

TRANSFER OPERATION. The transfer operation is a job usually supervised by a records manager if the organization has a centralized filing department. This individual oversees the operation of the files, establishes the transfer and retention procedures, and has the authority to dispose of obsolete records. If the size of the organization does not warrant a records manager position, one individual should be given authority to say what records should be transferred and what records, if any, should be destroyed.

In a business firm with formal transfer procedures, a records inventory would be consulted by the person in charge of the transfer. A *records inventory* is a statement of the kinds and quantity of records and folders in the files. This inventory would have been prepared when the filing system was installed, and updated when necessary.

The person in charge of transfer would need the following information in order to do an effective job:

1. The size and number of transfer file cabinets or boxes that are available.
2. The record that will be kept of transfer files.
3. Whether each department should select records for storage or destruction (under supervision) and box its files or whether this should be done by records specialists.
4. Whether each department should provide an inventory of files transferred or whether records specialists should prepare it.

Steps in the Transfer Process. A business may use the following steps in preparing for the transfer process:

1. Determine which files are ready to be transferred. This would depend on the transfer plan to be used.
2. Prepare new folders to replace those being transferred.
3. Assemble transfer boxes.
4. Remove the files from the file drawers and place them in the transfer boxes. (Authority should be in writing for any destroyed records.)
5. Inventory carefully the contents of each box to make a list of the contents for future reference and for the records of the storage area.
6. Label each box clearly and completely.

RECORDS STORAGE INDEX AND DESTRUCTION CONTROL CARD

RECORD TITLE Customer Ledgers									RECEIVED FROM Accounting		
DATE RECEIVED	FILE OR BOX NO.	CONTENTS				LOCATION			DATE TO DESTROY	DATE DES-TROYED	CERTIFIED BY
		ALPHABETIC NUMERIC		DATE		BLDG. OR ROOM	AISLE	SECTION			
		FROM	TO	FROM	TO						
1/25/81	168	1000	1025	3/16/80	3/31/80	238	B	10	1/25/86		

FORM 1607   RECORDS STORAGE INDEX AND DESTRUCTION CONTROL CARD   BB BANKERS BOX
records storage systems

On 1/25/81 the customer ledgers (recorded on the records inventory card on page 126) were received from the accounting department and placed in storage in the transfer storage location entered on the form. This form also authorizes destruction of the records five years later.

On the day of the transfer, a form is usually signed by the person releasing the files for storage and by the person accepting the records at the storage location.

Retrieving Records Which Have Been Stored. Provision has to be made for retrieval of records from a transfer storage area. When an office keeps detailed inventories of the files in storage, requested materials can be found quickly and easily. For example, refer to the illustration above: Customer Ledger 1000 is stored in Box 168. A diagram of the storage area would show the exact location of that box.

The contents of files may be stored on microfilm or microfiche. This process will be included in Chapter 13, "Specialized Systems," since the use of microforms has wider application than storage and transfer use.

METHODS OF DISPOSAL. Some records are destroyed by being fed through a specially designed shredding machine, which cuts them into narrow strips. Other methods of disposal are burning the records, selling them for scrap, or simply throwing them away. The confidential nature and the quantity of papers will usually determine the manner of disposal.

SURVEY OF COMPETENCIES

GENERAL REVIEW

The following questions will help you to reinforce your learning of the competencies included in this chapter:

1. Define the following terms:

   charge system   records retention
   records control   retention period
   records inventory   tickler file
   (Competency 1)

2. List and describe the elements of a charge system. (Competency 2)
3. How would charge systems differ between small offices and large offices? (Competency 2)
4. Why should requisition forms be completed even in small offices when records are removed from the files? (Competency 2)
5. Name three substitutes for a folder or record in the files. (Competency 3)
6. How do you locate a lost record? (Competency 4)
7. What questions would you ask when deciding how and when to transfer records? (Competency 5)
8. Name and describe three plans for the transfer of records. (Competency 6)
9. List the steps in the transfer process. (Competency 7)
10. How are records obtained from the storage files for use? (Competency 8)
11. What are the four methods of disposing of records? (Competency 9)

CASE PROBLEMS

1. Sandra Devich works for a small retail office supply store, and one of her duties is to charge out files. She would have no problem except that on Saturday mornings, when she is off, other employees have the habit of removing customer card records without making any notation about their removal; nor are the employees careful to replace the cards in the proper place in the file case when they are through. The consequence of this is that on Monday morning, when customers call to place orders, their records are often not available. Without the customer record, a purchase order for that customer may not be written. Of course, this delay does not promote good customer relations. Sandra, being in charge of the files, is held responsible. What can she do to protect her own record as a competent and responsible records manager? (Competencies 2, 3, 4)

2. What information should be on a routing slip attached to a letter which will be passed around the class by your instructor? The instructor's files would be the storage location. Describe two different methods which might be used. How could your instructor determine which class members had read the letter? (Competency 2)

3. Robert Maxwell is reluctant to transfer any records from his file drawers to the storage facility. He does not feel secure about his ability to retrieve any papers he may need at some time in the future. The records in his office tend to be used for a period of time until a project is finished; after that, only rarely are a project's records needed. What steps may be taken to assure Robert that there will be no problem in retrieving a record from the storage facility? (Competency 8)

4. Your employer does not like to throw anything out—ever. As a result, your files are hopelessly overcrowded with correspondence which is

as unnecessary now as the day it was filed there. Most of your activities include answering letters from customers who request price lists and brochures about your products. You feel that most of these letters could be disposed of immediately or at least within a very short period of time since those interested in the products fill out a purchase request. At that time a file is set up for active customers and is kept in the accounting department. In your office there are folders set up for each individual who writes requesting information. What do you suggest? (Competency 5)

If you have not mastered all of the competencies reviewed in the Survey, reread that part of the chapter which deals with the competency in question; then recheck your progress.

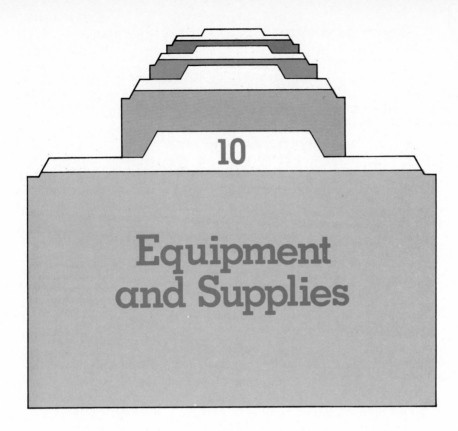

Equipment
and Supplies

COMPETENCIES

When you have completed this chapter, you will be able to:

1. Name sources for obtaining filing equipment and supplies.
2. List objectives of a records management system.
3. Name and describe seven kinds of equipment for correspondence files.
4. List and describe equipment for card files.
5. Name and describe types of records which have special equipment needs.
6. Describe important physical characteristics of the file drawer.
7. State how to determine how much file drawer space is needed.
8. Name accessories that are necessary or helpful to the filing process.
9. State factors to consider when selecting cards and business forms.

IMPORTANCE OF CAREFUL SELECTION

Dozens of manufacturers offer almost every conceivable type, size, price, and design of cabinets, supplies, and special equipment for housing and managing records. Made-to-order equipment is also available for unique systems. Office equipment exhibits, catalogs of manufacturers, office management magazines, and showrooms of stationers, business equipment dealers, and office furniture stores are excellent sources of up-to-date information. New filing products are placed on the market often. Office workers and supervisors who are concerned with records management should keep constantly in touch with new developments. Often the equipment and supplies suggest ways to solve filing problems and maintain an efficient filing system.

Carefully chosen filing equipment and supplies can serve the system in the following ways:

1. Saving time. This means that equipment and supplies must be designed so that those who handle records do not go through unnecessary motions. The biggest expense in filing is the cost of the people who do the work; any equipment or procedure that can save time will also save money.
2. Providing adequate protection of records. Some files should have locks to safeguard their contents; others should be fireproof. The importance of the records, then, needs to be considered when purchasing equipment.
3. Conserving space. Because of high rental for floor space, construction costs of new buildings, and maintenance expenses, files should be designed so that they do not take up more space than is absolutely necessary for an efficient system.

CORRESPONDENCE FILES

Correspondence files are usually made of steel and are available in a variety of types and grades of quality. The major types of correspondence files are vertical, open shelf, lateral, rotary, box, and tub.

VERTICAL FILES.   Vertical files are cabinets with usually four or five drawers the width of the long dimension of letter or legal folders. In these drawers the folders are placed behind each other about 26 to 30 inches deep. As these files are completely enclosed, they are sturdy and protect the contents. Many have locks and some, called *safes*, are made of special fireproof and protective materials with combination locks.

OPEN-SHELF FILES.   Open-shelf files look like steel bookcases and are flexible in size and arrangement. Folders are placed on the shelves the same way books are placed on a bookcase. Because these files use less space to store the same amount of materials as vertical file cabinets, they have become popular in recent years. For some businesses there has been as

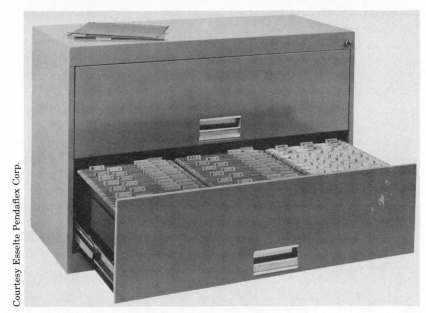

A popular filing cabinet found in many offices is the credenza style. It provides two file drawers for storing records as well as counter space.

It would be easy to find records in this well-organized open-shelf file with clearly marked alphabetic guides.

Equipment and Supplies 137

much as a 50 percent increase in the amount of storage space. Since one of the disadvantages of open-shelf files is the lack of protection of the records, some small units are available with sliding doors which will enclose both sides of the shelves and which may be locked to protect the files.

LATERAL FILES.   Lateral files are metal cabinet-type files, about 15 to 18 inches deep, in which the folders are placed in a bookshelf arrangement as on the open shelf files. After a receding door has been raised, the shelf pulls forward on rollers. Lateral files have the advantage of saving space as open-shelf filing does and the advantage of enclosing the files as vertical filing does. In addition to containing correspondence files, lateral files can be designed to include spaces for reference material, telephone, dictation and transcription equipment, and supplies so that these items are readily available but do not clutter the work area. Most lateral files are designed to be compatible with other modular furniture used in the office. They are available in many dimensions and are often used as dividers, credenzas, and counters.

ROTARY FILES.   Rotary files (also called *carousel files*) consist of round shelves attached to a center post by braces. The records to be filed are placed on the shelves as in open-shelf filing. Some shelves have built-in partitions to hold the records in place and upright. Rotary files are particularly useful for housing notebooks because notebooks form a pie-shaped arrangement. A rotary file is often used when several individuals in a work station need to use the group of file records; the file can be turned for easy access on all sides.

BOX FILES.   Box files are most commonly used for storage. The boxes are of low-cost steel or corrugated fiberboard. They can stand alone or be placed on shelves. Some types have steel devices which hold the boxes together in a stacked arrangement to form a bank of files. Box files are available in a variety of quality and size choices.

TUB FILES.   Tub files are containers which open at the top to expose records suspended in folders or in trays. Many tub files are relatively small and have the advantage of being movable from one work station to another. Larger tub files are automated and revolve to rotate the shelves to the workers.

POWER FILE UNITS.   Power file units operate automatically to move a particular shelf of files vertically to a convenient level for the user. The operator merely pushes a button to bring the desired shelf into working position. Within the unit, the files may be arranged as open-shelf files with side-tabbed folders or in small tubs or trays. Because the unit is enclosed, the power files can be locked for security. A power file is usually equipped with an electric eye or other safeguard device to scan the shelves for protruding materials which might interfere with the mechanical operation.

Because most business papers are standard 8½- by 11-inch size, the letter-size vertical cabinet is very common.

Rotating files move sections of shelf files horizontally to the user. Without leaving the desk, the file worker has access to one or more sections of the files. In this system, tracks are located on the floor and on the ceiling to secure the rollers for the file shelves.

CARD FILES

Vertical card files are made in a number of sizes. Some companies manufacture compartment inserts which can be used to change vertical file drawers into card files.

Rotary files may be set up for vertical or horizontal motion to facilitate access to cards.

Tub files may be large enough to hold a great many cards, checks, small forms, and so on. Small desk-top tub files can be used for reference, for work in progress, and to store materials.

Box files similar to those used for the storage of correspondence are available for cards of various sizes.

Power equipment similar to that used for correspondence files is available for card files.

Courtesy Xerox Corporation

An example of equipment designed for a special purpose is the Rolling T-Cart Storage unit. This transportable unit is used to store floppy disks used in word processing and small computer installations. The floppy disk fits into a vinyl pocket with a metal hanger. Colored signals alert the user to different kinds of stored information.

SPECIAL EQUIPMENT NEEDS

Some records are of such unique form that special equipment is designed to house them. These records include microforms (miniatures of office records), magnetic cards (cards with information recorded magnetically), and flexible (or floppy) disks. Equipment for them will be discussed along with the records themselves in Chapter 13.

LETTER-SIZE FILE DRAWER

CONSTRUCTION. The letter-size file drawer when full carries a load of 60 to 70 pounds. Therefore, this drawer should have telescoping slides to furnish support when it is fully extended. The slides should move on ball-bearing or nylon rollers so drawers can be opened and closed with one hand. The inside frame of the cabinet should be rigidly braced.

File drawers are not always completely filled, so records within them must be held upright by some device other than the back of the drawer. *Follower blocks,* or *compressors* as they are sometimes called, are used to support and to compress records. They move forward and backward in the file drawer, yet lock in the desired position to hold records. Followers should be strong but not so bulky that they occupy valuable filing space.

So that guides will not accidentally be lifted out of the drawer when folders are removed, there should be some means of anchoring the guides in place. Most file drawers have guide rods that are inserted through holes in one or more projections at the bottom or sides of the guides. This keeps guides in the drawer but permits them to move forward and backward along the rods.

If papers are packed too tightly in file drawers, they will become wrinkled and unsightly, folders and guides will be short-lived, and file workers will have difficulty removing and replacing records. To prevent such difficulties, some filing cabinets provide V-shaped working space. This working space is provided in some models by a drop front that eases the tension on the tops of the records when the drawer is opened and compresses the records when the drawer is closed.

DETERMINING DRAWER SPACE NEEDS. In deciding how many drawers or cabinets are needed, it is necessary to determine the quantity of material to be filed. The chart shown below can then be used to estimate the number of inches (measured from front to back inside the drawer) of filing space that will be needed.

CORRESPONDENCE FILING SPACE CHART

Item	Average Filing Space Required
175 pieces of correspondence	$1''$
25 guides (medium weight)	$\frac{7}{8}''$
100 individual folders (medium weight)	$2\frac{1}{4}''$
25 miscellaneous folders (medium weight)	$\frac{1}{2}''$

By dividing into this figure the filing inches in one drawer, the number of file drawers needed will be known. Correspondence files have between 24 and 27 inches of filing space, but about 4 inches should be subtracted for working space. For example, if the chart shows that the filed materials will occupy 1,000 inches, and there are 24 inches of filing space in each drawer of the cabinets to be purchased, then the number of cabinets that will be needed is figured as follows:

Filing inches in each drawer	24
Minus inches allowed for working space	−4
Inches of space to be used in each drawer	20
Inches of space all records will use	1,000
Divide by space to be used in each drawer	$1,000 \div 20 = 50$ drawers
Number of drawers needed	50 drawers ÷ 4 or 5 =
Number of cabinets is then figured by dividing number of drawers per cabinet into number needed.	13 four-drawer or 10 five-drawer cabinets

GUIDES. Guides are the key to efficient vertical filing. Without them, records will not stand upright properly in the drawer. Guides also serve as signposts to speed finding and filing. The number of guides, the tab size and position, and the quality of construction depend on the filing system being used. They may be purchased in all standard correspondence drawer sizes as well as for drawers used in special systems, such as bank, hospital, and insurance company files. Guides made of manila stock or index bristol are inexpensive and will serve in transfer files or temporary card files. In active files, however, guides made of pressboard or fiber should be used. A standard 25-point (0.025-inch) thickness of pressboard is durable and rigid enough to support records, yet flexible enough to resist dog-earing or breaking. In some card systems, guides made of plastic or lightweight metal are used.

Guides are produced with the tab or upper-edge projection in various sizes (cuts) and positions so that they can be adapted to any system. The tabs may be simply an extension of the guide with the caption printed or with a blank space for a label. Some tabs of this type are reinforced with transparent plastic. High-quality guides, however, have metal or plastic tabs that are riveted to the body of the guide. Such tabs usually have a slot for the insertion of a caption label under a transparent plastic window.

There are a number of other guide features and accessories. Angular tabs are slanted back for good visibility and are especially helpful in lower file drawers. There are even tabs that magnify the guide caption. Separate plastic tabs can be purchased in long strips and cut to the desired size for attachment to guides in any position. These may be used to replace broken tabs or to provide additional captions. Good-quality guides have metal-reinforced guide rod projections. As with filing cabinets, the best-quality guides with the most useful features are usually worth the extra money because they give lasting and efficient service.

GUIDES AND TABS OF VARYING DESIGN

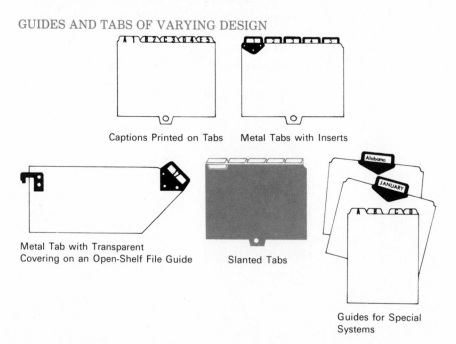

Captions Printed on Tabs   Metal Tabs with Inserts

Metal Tab with Transparent
Covering on an Open-Shelf File Guide   Slanted Tabs

Guides for Special
Systems

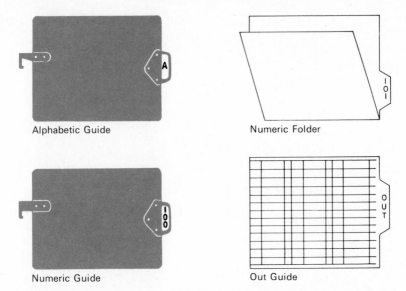

Alphabetic Guide

Numeric Folder

Numeric Guide

Out Guide

FOLDERS. Durable folders that have a minimum of thickness and a smooth surface are needed for active correspondence files. As is true with guides, folders are available in several styles and types of materials. For average use, manila and kraft folders provide good service and can be purchased in several weights; the choice should depend upon the type and extent of handling. Plastic folders have the advantages of reusability and ease of filing. For bulky papers or for very heavy handling, fiber or pressboard folders with cloth expansion hinges at the bottom should be used. For checks and other small business forms, transparent plastic folders may be the most appropriate.

Some folders have a double thickness along the top, which adds to their life span without increasing the bulk of the file drawer. Folders that are scored along the bottom of the front flap can be expanded neatly. As the number of papers increases, a new fold is made along one of the scores. This flattens the bottom and permits all records to stand evenly and squarely on their edges.

Several types of folders are designed for special needs. File pockets, also called envelope folders, are used for materials that are especially bulky or that are frequently taken away from the files. For case histories, medical records, and personnel records, folders that have dividers or compartments within them are frequently used. For follow-up work, folders with adjustable date signals are popular. Other folders that are available have built-in paper fasteners to keep records from accidentally sliding out.

Folder tabs are obtainable in nearly any cut or position desired. Tabs are generally an extension of the folder itself, but pressboard and fiber folders usually have metal or plastic tabs. For open-shelf files, tabs are on the side of guides and folders instead of the top.

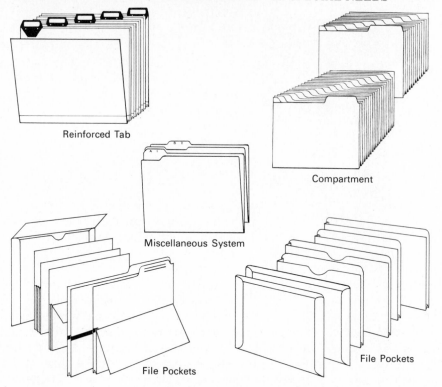

Reinforced Tab

Compartment

Miscellaneous System

File Pockets

File Pockets

Suspended, or *hanging,* folders are supported from their top edges by a metal frame within the file drawer. They do not rest on the bottom of the drawer. These folders save space because the follower blocks and guides can be eliminated (attachable tabs on the front of the folders can be used in the place of conventional guides). Suspended folders usually have a neat appearance and permit easy storage and removal of records.

OTHER FILE DRAWER ACCESSORIES. Folder, guide, and drawer labels may be purchased in several styles. One of the most popular is the self-adhesive type, which requires no moistening. Labels can be bought printed or blank, in strips or rolls, with colors or plain.

Colored signals are useful and can be positioned along the top edges of folders and guides for classification purposes. Signals are also used frequently with visible equipment. They can be fixed or movable and are constructed of paper, plastic, or metal.

Standard printed forms, such as cross-reference sheets, are often made to order for customers by the filing equipment companies. Some companies will print easy-to-read captions on individual folder tabs from a list of names submitted by the customer.

Other equipment that will add to filing efficiency includes the following: files stools to make working at lower drawers comfortable, movable shelves to allow workers to use both hands while filing, drawer dividers to separate records conveniently, sorting devices to speed the preliminary arranging of records, and several types of date stamps, trays, and stands.

For help in selecting equipment and supplies, it is a good idea to have a filing catalog handy for reference. For comparison purposes, two or more filing equipment companies should be consulted whenever a large purchase is to be made. These companies have the experience and desire to be helpful not only in providing equipment and supplies but also in helping to design a filing system that will bring top efficiency and satisfaction. The quality of this advisory service is an important factor to consider when deciding from what dealer to buy equipment and supplies.

SELECTING CARDS AND BUSINESS FORMS

A purchasing agent, a records manager, or, in a small office, a secretary or accountant may purchase filing supplies. Since card records and business forms are of great importance in carrying out office responsibilities, they are discussed in detail below.

CARDS. The selection of cards to be purchased for both vertical and visible card files is generally the job of the file and records worker or supervisor. "What will the card be used for?" is the key question that should be answered first, not "How much do the cards cost?" The cost of the most expensive cards available is a small fraction of the cost of maintaining them as records. Once their use has been determined, the characteristics of the card needed will depend on:

1. Whether the card will be kept as a permanent or as a temporary record.
2. Whether the record will be handled frequently or infrequently.
3. Whether the card will have a transparent covering for protection or be unprotected.
4. Whether the card will be used for posting (by hand or machine) or for an index.
5. Whether or not the card will be used for classifying items by its color.

A card record that will be kept permanently or that will be handled frequently or be unprotected should, of course, be heavy and of very high quality. Inexpensive, lighter-weight cards may be purchased for temporary, seldom-handled, or protected card records. Various weights of file cards are available—light, medium, heavy, and extra-heavy. Various proportions of sulphite and fiber content determine the durability of the cards. A card with a high fiber content is more durable (and more expensive) than a card with a high sulphite content. For posted card records, the relative smoothness of the surface of a card, known as its *finish,* is important. Several finishes are available, from rough to very smooth and glossy, which are best suited to hand and machine posting, respectively.

Card records are sometimes protected by transparent plastic coverings from soiling, bending, and deteriorating. In many visible files the visible edge of the card, because it is most frequently handled, is protected by a clear plastic strip. In vertical card files, cards that are often referred to are sometimes enclosed entirely in cellophane. A device being used in business for permanently enclosing records in clear plastic is the *laminating machine*. A record is fed into the machine, and a plastic coating seals both sides of the record.

In order to classify certain categories in a card file, such as local and out-of-town customers, cards of various colors are often used—perhaps green cards for local customers and blue cards for out-of-town customers. Not only are dozens of solid colors available, but cards may also be purchased with vertical or horizontal stripes. Items are classified according to the color, width, and position of the colored stripes on the cards.

BUSINESS FORMS.   Forms requiring other than standard-size filing cabinets can prove to be inefficient because of the extra cost of the equipment. Even legal-size cabinets cost more and occupy more space than standard letter-size ones. A small form can become hidden and difficult to find when filed with larger records. Likewise, a large form can take extra space and slow down file searching when it is folded to standard letter-size dimensions. Therefore, a form should usually be designed to have the same dimensions as the other records with which it will be stored.

Standard paper-mill sizes should also be considered before deciding on the size of a particular form. This will ensure minimum waste and lowest cost per form. The printer should be consulted for this information.

SURVEY OF COMPETENCIES

GENERAL REVIEW

The following questions will help you to reinforce your learning of the competencies included in this chapter.

1. Where can you obtain information about filing equipment and supplies? (Competency 1)
2. What are the objectives of an efficient records management system? (Competency 2)
3. Name and describe the seven kinds of equipment used for storing correspondence. (Competency 3)
4. List and describe the equipment used for card files. Which of these is similar to equipment used for correspondence? Which would not be suitable for correspondence? (Competency 4)
5. What are some records that have special equipment needs? How are these records stored? (Competency 5)
6. What are the important physical characteristics of the file drawer? (Competency 6)

7. How do you decide how many file drawers to purchase when buying new equipment? (Competency 7)

8. What are follower blocks? What are guide rods? (Competency 6)

9. What functions do guides serve? What are some different features of guides? (Competency 8)

10. What are some of the various types of folders available? (Competency 8)

11. What other accessories are necessary and helpful to the filing process? (Competency 8)

12. What questions need to be asked when determining the kind of cards to select for card records? What does laminating do for card records? (Competency 9)

13. What do you need to consider when selecting business forms? (Competency 9)

CASE PROBLEMS

1. After Josephine Marshall retired she left her business to her nephew, Marshall Foresight. Marshall has decided to renovate the offices and would like to update the filing equipment. However, he does not know what equipment is available nor what it should do to be effective. He asks your advice. How can you help? (Competencies 1, 3, 4, 8)

2. When you begin working for an office that has vertical files, you find some difficulties with the equipment. The drawers are too crowded and you cannot pull out folders easily. There are only two or three guides in each drawer, and captions are typed or written directly on the folder tabs. One of your job duties is to make suggestions and implement them to make the filing system easier to work with. Describe what you plan to do. (Competencies 2, 3, 6, 8)

3. Although records are transferred as often as feasible, the active files of the Dawson Company are too crowded for efficient use. Additional floor space is not available for file cabinets. The lease on the present quarters still has three years to run. How would you provide more file space? (Competencies 3, 6, 8)

4. Carl Porter mentions to his employer, the owner of a travel bureau, that there must be a faster and more efficient way of getting folders and other information for people making personal inquiries. At present he has to walk to the files and storage cabinets in the rear of the office. What would you suggest? (Competencies 3, 5)

5. Paul Smith has to make frequent use of a large card file. He refers to it to obtain information that requires very little writing. What would you suggest to eliminate the need for his removing the card from the drawer, walking to a desk to record the information, and then returning to reinsert the card in the file? (Competencies 4, 5)

If you have not mastered all of the competencies reviewed in the Survey, reread that part of the chapter which deals with the competency in question; then recheck your progress.

11

Setting Up
a Work Station

COMPETENCIES

When you have completed this chapter you will be able to:

1. Define the term *work station*.
2. Compare and contrast the landscaped office and the traditional office.
3. List supplies commonly kept in and on the desk.
4. List reference materials which help you on the job.
5. List and describe reminder and follow-up files that you can use.
6. Describe how you set priorities for your work in the office.

WHAT IS A WORK STATION?

Your work station in the office is the area where you perform your duties. A work station usually consists of a desk, chair, shelves or bookcase, files, typewriter, and all the supplies necessary to do your job. You may share parts of your work station—the files, for example—with other individuals in the office. Generally speaking, *work station* means the physical equipment and supplies arranged so that you can carry out your daily work routine in an efficient way.

Many years ago the work station was a rolltop desk and chair or a high stool for working at a counter. Now offices have metal furniture with sleek lines, laminated plastic surfaces in various colors, and modular components that can be added to rearrange work areas according to need.

TYPES OF OFFICE LAYOUTS

There are two basic types of office layouts: the traditional, or enclosed, office and the landscaped, or open, office.

The traditional office arrangement has enclosed cubicles or rooms of various sizes in which work stations of one or more individuals are set up. The size of the office, the location, the number of individuals who share the office, the view (if there *is* a window!), and the furnishings are all status symbols within the organizational structure of the business.

Because of rising salaries and the division of labor made possible by word processing equipment, not many executives work on a one-to-one basis with a secretary. Usually a secretary works for several individuals, and some tasks ordinarily handled by a secretary are sent to support services, such as a word processing center, in other locations. This division of responsibility has led to the landscaped office which features an open area partitioned by furniture and dividers of various heights for privacy. With this type of office arrangement, management is able to place more employees in the space available than if the traditional office arrangement were used.

The introduction of word processing machines and computers into the office has led to the need to rearrange the office layout to cut down on noise. Landscaped offices are usually carpeted and have dividers made of sound-proofing materials to absorb the noise of the machines and voices.

A variation of both the landscaped and the traditional office is the use of cubicles with movable partitions.

YOUR WORK AREA

Whatever the arrangement of your office, the immediate area where you work—your desk, files, bookcase, whatever is yours to use to perform your duties—is a reflection of you as an employee. You should be conscious of the appearance you create as you work and as you leave your desk at the end of the day. Following are some questions you can ask yourself to see if you are making the best use of your work station.

Are materials put away? Do you work on one task at a time and keep other items neatly arranged? Do you keep distractions away from what you are doing? Do you have reference materials within easy reach? Do you have enough supplies on hand so that you do not have to make frequent trips for supplies? Do you combine trips away from your desk? Do you have pencil and paper ready to take notes? The diagram on page 151 illustrating arrangements for work and supplies on a desk may help you to organize your work area.

DESK SUPPLIES. Most desks are constructed to allow for an efficient arrangement of supplies. Everyday paper supplies—stationery, onionskin, and carbon paper—can be placed in a rack in a drawer (or other closed compartment) of the desk. Most desks have a shallow drawer for supplies which must be kept handy, such as scissors, stapler and staples, paper clips, cellophane tape, rubber stamps and stamp pad, and glue. If new folders and cards need to be set up often for the filing system, these items should also be kept in the desk.

Another desk drawer may be convenient to hold vertical files of business forms and records needed for daily reference.

Heavy or bulky items that are not convenient to store inside can be kept on the desk. A telephone should be placed for convenient reach, and telephone information slips or notepaper should be handy for making notes on calls. Other top-of-desk items might include an appointment calendar, a card file, a pencil cup, baskets or trays for incoming and outgoing papers, a time stamp, and reference materials. The most commonly used reference materials are a telephone book, a company directory, a dictionary, an employee's handbook, and an office procedures manual.

REMINDER AND FOLLOW-UP FILES. There are several files which are used for making sure that the work for which you are responsible gets done on time. You will need to select those files which best meet your particular needs. Although some of the following files may be used interchangeably, each has its own characteristics:

1. *Chronological file*. This file holds items in order by date, usually for a 1-month period, with days of the month 1 to 31 used as captions for folders or for the dividers in an accordian file. Items are placed behind the date on which some action must be taken. The file is then checked each day and the action is taken, or a decision is made to postpone the action and the item is moved to a new date. (Some items, such as information or reminders, can be discarded after their purpose has been served.) Items which would fall on weekends or holidays should be moved forward to the prior working day.

2. *Correspondence file*. This file contains model letters and is particularly helpful to the newcomer on the job since it provides a reference to the style, tone, and content of letters which have been written. Because it contains copies of correspondence, it may be used in the same way as the reading file (see item 6).

3. *Follow-up file*. This file may be, but is not necessarily, arranged by date (chronologically). It may also have an alphabetic arrangement. It contains work you need to check on at a later date. This work may extend over a period of time or it may be of short duration and then discarded or filed when action has been taken or notice of action has been received. You may be awaiting responses from several individuals you have invited to a meeting to be held next month. As you receive this information, you check it off and proceed with the rest of your plans. This sort of task does not warrant the setting up of a special folder.

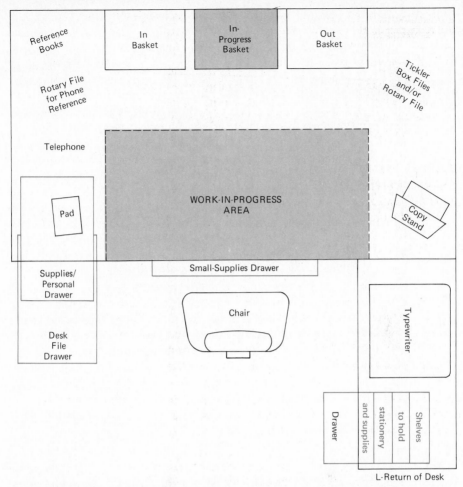

Reference Books

In Basket

In-Progress Basket

Out Basket

Rotary File for Phone Reference

Tickler Box Files and/or Rotary File

Telephone

Pad

WORK-IN-PROGRESS AREA

Copy Stand

Small-Supplies Drawer

Supplies/ Personal Drawer

Chair

Typewriter

Desk File Drawer

Drawer | and supplies | stationery | to hold | Shelves

L-Return of Desk

For efficient daily work routine, plan where to place the materials you need, and keep them in order.

4. *Hold-for-answer file.* This file contains carbons or copies of letters you have written requesting information or notes you have made for which you are awaiting a response. These items should be handled as replies are received—either filed, used, or placed in a different follow-up folder.

5. *Pending file.* This file contains matters which are not yet completed—because you are waiting for information, you have not yet finished necessary details, it is not something of top priority but something that needs to be done, or it is a bright idea to work on in your spare time. The pending file can be used for a combination of work items or for a specific job in progress.

6. *Reading file.* This file contains a chronological collection of extra carbon copies of correspondence you have sent out of the office during a specific period of time. The length of time will vary according to the quantity of correspondence. Since you can often

remember sending a letter to someone last week, the reading file is a handy reference particularly if it will save time by not requiring material from a centralized filing location.

7. *Suspense file.* This file is similar to a chronological file because it contains folders by date, one for each day of the month, by month, and by year. As items are noted which will come up in the future, the information is placed in the appropriate folder. The difference between the suspense file and the chronological file is that suspense file items require some definite action to be taken. For example, your office may loan materials to employees. These materials must be returned when due. The suspense file notation should demand that a follow-up notice be sent.

8. *Tickler card file.* This file is handy for following up on any items which can conveniently be recorded on small cards. Notations may be made about bills to pay, dates to remember, meetings to attend, and preparations to be made for big jobs coming up. These cards are usually set up by day with dividers for the days of the month and months of the year as in chronological filing.

9. *Tickler folder file.* This file operates in the same manner as the tickler card file, but the items are too large to be placed on a card. It is particularly useful for items which may serve as reminders or information only and then can be disposed of after use.

10. *Work-in-progress file.* This file contains several projects (or one large project) which are not yet finished and which need periodic attention until completed. All the details for making a large report, for example, would be kept in this file until it was finished. The report would then be filed where appropriate.

All these files are kept in the desk or within easy reach. The tickler card file may be kept on top of the desk or in a small drawer; the folder files may be kept in a desk file drawer or a desk-top organizer.

SETTING PRIORITIES

Setting priorities means deciding the order of urgency of jobs to be done. The most important or the most urgent work is assigned top priority and must be done first. Other tasks are then done according to their importance. In the office routine you will find you have work to do that is urgent or "rush," work that is important, work that is routine or "necessary," and work that is done only when you have spare time. To be an effective worker, you need to set goals for work to be accomplished each day and to organize your time to meet those goals.

"TO DO" LIST. One of the best ways to keep track of work which needs to be done is to keep a "To Do" list. This is a list of all the items that need attention within the next day or so. Items which need attention in the future should be noted on a calendar or filed in one of your follow-up files.

A clear working space and an uncluttered desk improve efficiency.

The "To Do" list is a way to organize your workday, making sure that the most important items get done while still keeping track of other tasks which are important. As items are completed, cross them off your list. You will need to rewrite the list periodically, possibly once or twice a day. This allows you time to think about what you have to do and plan ahead.

DESK TRAYS.   On your desk you will probably have containers to hold work which will be brought to you by others and to hold work you have completed which will be picked up by others. These containers are usually metal or plastic trays labeled *in* and *out* baskets. You may also have a *hold* basket for work in progress. Work which you receive during the day may affect priorities you have already set and thus require you to reorganize your "To Do" list.

INDIVIDUALIZING YOUR WORK STATION

Your work station is a reflection of you as a person and your work habits. A neat, tidy desk shows that you are careful, organized, and efficient. A messy desk can usually be improved by finding a place to keep items which you are not using. You can show your individuality by placing a houseplant or two on or near your desk. Many landscaped offices use plants for atmosphere and decoration. There are also many small accessories which can be used for practical and decorative purposes. A paperweight can hold down your "To Do" list as well as add a note of color to your surroundings. A bright cup can be used to hold pens and pencils. Your work station is where you spend the majority of your working day. Use this area to add a touch of yourself to the office.

SURVEY OF COMPETENCIES

GENERAL REVIEW

The following questions will help you to reinforce your learning of the competencies included in this chapter.

1. What is a work station?   (Competency 1)
2. What are the differences between the landscaped office and the traditional office? Why has the landscaped office become popular?   (Competency 2)
3. Name supplies that you will need to use.   (Competency 3)
4. What are reference materials that will help you on the job?   (Competency 4)
5. What are the different reminder and follow-up file systems that you might use on the job?   (Competency 5)
6. Describe how you set priorities for your work in the office.   (Competency 6)

CASE PROBLEMS

1. Having reference books to use in the office will help you do your job better. Will any of the textbooks you have used in your classes be appropriate to use on the job? What reference materials do you think your employer will provide for you? What reference materials might you wish to obtain yourself?   (Competency 4)
2. You have been hired by Mr. Jacobsen to work in his new office. He asks you for a list of supplies you will need for your desk. What items will you include?   (Competency 3)
3. You have been working several months for Dr. Alberta Kincaid, a noted author and lecturer. Dr. Kincaid makes commitments months in advance for speaking engagements. You find that the dates for these talks sneak up on you. You constantly have to look through your appointment book and hold basket for materials you need to prepare for her speeches as well as check on the travel arrangements, some of which must be booked months in advance. Of the reminder and follow-up files described in this chapter, which would be the most appropriate for your use? Describe how you will set up your files.   (Competencies 5, 6)
4. As administrative assistant for Michael Smith, a real estate agent, you find that you are tired at the end of each day because you cannot keep up with all the details of your job. You feel you could get more done if you were more organized. What advice is given in this chapter to help you?   (Competencies 1, 3, 4, 5, 6)

If you have not mastered all of the competencies reviewed in the Survey, reread that part of the chapter which deals with the competency in question; then recheck your progress.

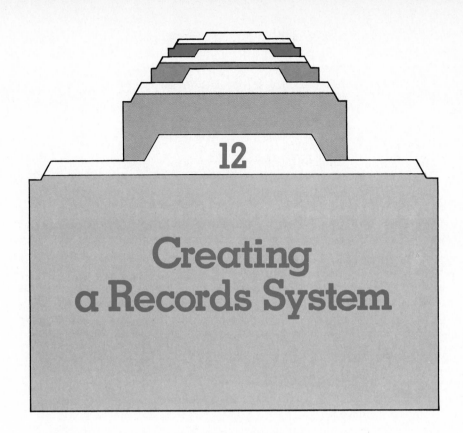

12

Creating a Records System

COMPETENCIES

When you have completed this chapter, you will be able to:

1. List questions which should be asked to analyze the needs of a business.
2. Define the terms *centralized* and *decentralized* and tell how these organization plans affect where the files are kept.
3. List the steps to be followed when setting up a file system.
4. Describe how you make changes in an existing filing system.
5. List the parts of a procedures manual.
6. Give two examples of use of color and numbers in "home-made" filing systems.
7. Describe two variations of filing procedures which are used by small businesses.

ANALYZING THE NEEDS OF THE BUSINESS

Because businesses make plans for continued growth, records management systems must be flexible to meet changing needs. Creation of new office positions, installation of modern automated equipment, and the constant need to keep costs under control are among current business concerns that affect records management.

The following questions are important in analyzing the needs of the business:

What is the nature of the business or organization?
How is the business organized?
What is the format of the records to be kept?
Where are the files located?
What retention schedule applies to the business?

NATURE OF THE BUSINESS.   The main point of any filing system is *retrieval*. Information is stored because it is needed, and of course it is of no use if it cannot be located and retrieved when it is needed. Whatever system allows the most efficient retrieval will vary according to the nature of the business. For example, in a medical office where several staff members (a receptionist, nurse, physician, bookeeper) consult one set of files, it is important to avoid misfiling records. Many medical offices use a color-coded numeric system because they help to prevent misfiling and because, if a record should be misfiled, the color coding makes it easy to spot.

A professor would probably choose a subject system. The name of a course may be one of the primary guides, and folders might be opened to hold reference materials for each unit, tests, worksheets, and other papers related to that course.

These are just two examples to illustrate that the filing system of any business or organization should be adapted so that it best serves the retrieval of the records.

CENTRALIZED OR DECENTRALIZED FILES.   *Centralized files* are files of records in one location under the supervision of one person or one department. *Decentralized files* are files located in the various departments where they are used. Variations of both arrangements are possible. A business may establish one set of procedures that applies to all files in various locations. The procedures are centralized—or under one control—but the actual files are decentralized. Another variation is to store in a central location the files that are needed across-the-board—or by all departments of the business—and to store in department locations the records that are needed by department employees only. In most businesses, a few files are always decentralized because they are needed for daily routine at individual work stations.

The space that is available, the personnel who need to consult the records, the work flow from one department to another, the number of records, and the equipment needed to store them—all these factors enter into the decision about whether files should be centralized or decentralized.

FORMAT OF THE RECORDS.   Records are of many different sizes and shapes and may be made of paper or other materials. For example, records may be

Floppy disks are now found in many offices because of the growing use of word/information processing equipment. This binder with cushioned pockets protects the disks. An index on the back is used to locate a particular disk.

typed on 8½- by 11-inch paper or on 5 by 3 cards; records may be on magnetic tape or magnetic cards; records may be on microfiche or aperture cards. A traditional file cabinet obviously does not serve all these storage needs. You need to survey the format of the records to be stored and select the equipment that is best for the job.

LOCATION OF FILES. Decisions about where to store records are not usually determined by the desires of the employees who use them. In centralized files, one central location is reserved by administrative managers who plan the use of space in the office. In decentralized files, the cost of space and equipment may dictate location. File cabinets may double as partitions between work stations in an open office to save the cost of partitions. Some records may be preserved on microfilm or computer tapes to save space.

If responsibility for planning the arrangement of files is assigned to you, one way to approach this responsibility is to use a *template* of standard office equipment sizes to make a scale drawing of the area and to place the furniture and equipment on this scale drawing.

ESSENTIAL RECORDS. You learned in Chapter 9 that decisions about what records need to be stored and how long they should be kept are affected by federal and state legislation on taxes and insurance and fair employment. Records of historical value and records that may be needed in case of litigation are also essential. In addition, of course, records are needed to carry on the business. These and other requirements must be considered in selecting or creating a records system for a business or organization.

SETTING UP A FILE SYSTEM

It is possible that an office worker may be asked to set up a file system for a small business—perhaps a new business such as a real estate office, insurance agency, doctor's office, lawyer's office, or employment agency. If you find yourself in a position where you are asked to assume this responsibility, this list of steps may be helpful to you.

1. Analyze the needs of the office.
   a. What is the type of business?
   b. What kinds of records will the business have?
   c. What filing systems are used by other offices that handle the same kinds of papers?
   d. What is the expected volume of records? (Make allowance for expansion and proper distribution.)
   e. What factors need to be considered for flexibility as the business grows?
2. Select a system based on your answers to the questions that are listed in item 1. Consult an office supplier and salespersons for commercial systems and supplies available.
3. Plan the auxiliary systems you will need, such as subject files for miscellaneous materials and follow-up files for follow-up activities.
4. Implement the system.
5. Evaluate how the system is working.
6. Make necessary revisions.
7. Develop a manual for others to follow and as a reminder for yourself.

By following these steps, you can start a new filing system with some degree of confidence that your choice will work.

REVISING AND UPDATING AN EXISTING SYSTEM

As a business grows and changes, the filing system and records management functions of the office will need to be revised and changed. As you work with the files, you may be able to make suggestions to your supervisor that will make your job easier or save you time. To improve your performance in the handling of records is a part of your job.

ANALYSIS OF THE SYSTEM.   If the business needs to make major revisions of the filing system, a procedure should be followed similar to that of setting up an entirely new system. Since changing an existing system will cost a great deal of money, careful thought and planning must go into the decision to make the change. There will be costs not only for new equipment and supplies but also for the time that employees must spend making the change.

Analysis of what is wrong with the existing system may disclose that with a few modifications the filing system can function more efficiently. For example, a simple situation such as file drawers being too crowded may create problems in retrieval. You feel that more equipment is the solution. Before you buy equipment consider the following questions: What materials are making the file drawer crowded? Check the contents of several folders in each drawer. Do they contain papers which could be transferred or destroyed? Are all the drawers crowded, or only a few? Would moving some files result in more even distribution? Should you change your transfer plan to remove more inactive files sooner? Would checking files to remove nonessential paperwork as the files are being used improve your situation? Would converting to open-shelf files give you more filing space in a smaller area? You can see that a simple situation such as overcrowded files may be resolved in one of several ways.

When you approach the subject of changing an existing system, ask those who use the files what problems they encounter. The input of others will accomplish two things: (1) others may have some ideas or solutions based on practical experience which you had not thought of, and (2) soliciting their opinions will help in securing their cooperation later on when the changes are made.

When you make more than a small change, do it by parts. Try to revise a shelf, drawer, or other small area to see (1) how much time is involved in making the revision, (2) what other decisions and changes may need to be made, and (3) does the change really work: is it better than what you had before? When you have decided that what is new is really better, finish the job.

As with the new system, revisions need to be evaluated. Make notes of problems you encounter as well as questions and problems others may have had. Make revisions as necessary. And develop a procedures manual for yourself and others.

PROCEDURES MANUAL. Your procedures manual should describe the filing system and include all pertinent information to enable others to use the system efficiently. It should contain, but may not be limited to, the following information:

1. A brief but basic description of the system and how it works: alphabetic, subject, numeric, geographic, or any combination. Be sure to describe the cross-referencing system you are using.
2. Practical information: where the supplies are located, how to set up a new folder. One sure way to cause chaos in the office is to leave materials which should be in the files lying around because no one knows how to get them into the system.
3. An explanation of the charge-out and follow-up systems.
4. How the regular filing is to be done: who does it, when, and what steps are to be followed.

5. The plan for transfer and disposal. Include the name of the person who has the authority for these activities.
6. The auxiliary systems necessary to complete the total picture, such as subject files for miscellaneous items, card files, follow-up files, indexes, and registers for numeric filing.

Your procedures manual should be a "cookbook" for those who may need to work with the system when you are busy or absent. It need not be in great detail, but it should be understandable to others in the office. You may feel you are making yourself indispensable by controlling the filing system, but, in fact, others will appreciate your thoughtfulness in making the system easy for them to use.

USING COLOR AND NUMBERS

Commercial color-coded systems and numbered systems are discussed in the next chapter. There are ways to use color and numbers in your "home-made" or noncommercial system. For example, a lawyer's secretary might want to color-code folders for divorce cases, real estate transactions, criminal cases, and civil cases. Marking pens of different colors can be used to draw a line along the top of the file folder tab and along the top of the index card for the card file. Blue might indicate divorce; red, real estate; green, criminal cases; yellow, civil cases.

To make your numeric system, you may decide to give each letter of the alphabet a number. You could decide to file by numbers using the first and second letters of the first indexing unit and the first letter of the second indexing unit, thus giving you three separate numbers to file the folder under. Using *1* for *A, 2* for *B, 3* for *C,* and so forth, you would file *John E. Appleseed* using the numbers *1/16/10* (*A* is *1, P* is *16,* and *J* is *10*).

VARIATIONS IN A STANDARD FORM

Small businesses tend to have filing systems with special adaptations that big businesses cannot allow in their more complex systems. A furniture rental business may file its numbered contracts in reverse order with the largest (most recently used) number on top. Contract number 198 would be in front of 197. The rationale for this procedure is that the last one written will probably need to be used again soon for reference. Those individuals whose contracts are older have had their questions answered, their items delivered, and so forth. Another example is the use of telephone numbers to file catalog orders for customers who will be coming in to pick up those orders. The last digit of the phone number is used for a major division. This is then divided according to the letters of the alphabet. For example, *Susan Roberts* (telephone number 555-3312) would be filed under *R* in the major division *2.*

Although there are general principles and rules which apply to all systems, these may be adapted to the preferences of the individuals in charge and the needs of the particular business, as long as those variations are known and understood by the users of the system.

SURVEY OF COMPETENCIES

GENERAL REVIEW

The following questions will help you to reinforce your learning of the competencies included in this chapter.

1. What questions should be asked to analyze the needs of the business? (Competency 1)
2. What does *centralized* mean? *Decentralized?* (Competency 2)
3. What are the steps to be followed in setting up a file system? (Competency 3)
4. How do you revise or update an existing system? (Competency 4)
5. What is a procedures manual? What do you need to include in it? (Competency 5)
6. How can you use colors and numbers in making your own file system? (Competency 6)
7. What are two variations of filing procedures used by small businesses? (Competency 7)

CASE PROBLEMS

1. Mary Smith is excited about her new job working for a doctor who is just setting up practice. She must set up the filing system and is unsure where to start. What advice can you give her? (Competencies 1, 3, 5, 6, 7)
2. Your mother keeps complaining that she cannot find records she needs. Everything is kept in two cardboard boxes in the attic. What have you learned in this chapter (and thus far in this textbook) that would help your mother? (Competencies 1, 3, 4)
3. You work in an office which has decentralized files. You find that you need to go to other departments to find information you need about customers, such as credit information from the billing department and frequently ordered items from the purchasing department. Would centralized files help your situation? (Competency 2)

If you have not mastered all of the competencies reviewed in the Survey, reread that part of the chapter which deals with the competency in question; then recheck your progress.

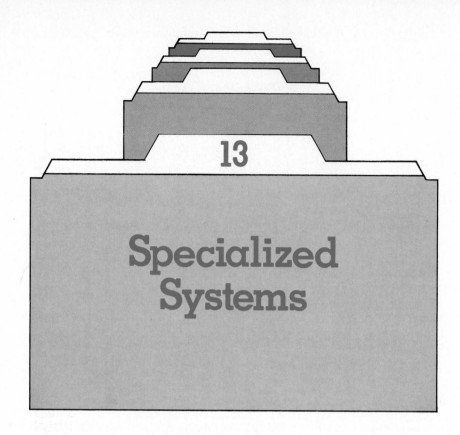

Specialized
Systems

When you have completed this chapter, you will be able to:

1. List four major developments in specialized systems being used in filing and records management.
2. List and briefly describe the three formats used for color-coded alphabetic and numeric systems.
3. State why color systems are used and state two differences between these systems and the alphabetic and numeric filing systems previously outlined.
4. Define the following terms: *micrographics, microform, microimages, microfilm, microfiche, aperture cards, micropublishing, microrepublishing, microfacsimile, CAR,* and *COM.*
5. List the advantages and disadvantages of microfilm and microfiche.
6. List the advantages of automated filing units.
7. List the advantages of a paperless office.
8. Explain why a knowledge of filing basics is extremely important when working with computers.
9. List some of the traditional items of records management equipment that will not appear in the office of the future.

CHARACTERISTICS OF SPECIALIZED SYSTEMS

You have studied the basic filing systems for alphabetic, numeric, subject, and geographic filing. These systems provide for storing and retrieving records, using standard equipment for filing procedures, including equipment for reproduction of records, storage, and retrieval. Specialized systems serve the same functions; however, they are designed and constructed by office equipment manufacturers and are often part of the technological change in the office along with computers and word processing equipment.

Four major developments in the office are related to specialized systems. These are (1) color-coded filing systems, (2) micrographics, (3) computer-assisted retrieval and computer output microfilm, and (4) automated retrieval equipment.

COLOR-CODED SYSTEMS

Color-coded systems are designed to prevent misfiling and speed the location of records. There are three basic formats used for color systems: (1) the folder may be a distinctive color, (2) the label may be a distinctive color, or (3) the folder may have one or more bars of color which identify its location in the file. The first two formats may be commercially made or may be office-made as described in Chapter 12. The third system is usually obtained from a vendor of filing systems.

Colored folders are used for specific purposes. For example, an office might put all financial records in yellow folders, all contracts in green folders, all personnel records in blue folders, and so on, to identify the contents. Some systems use a specific color, for example, green for the first 1,000 folders, blue for the second 1,000 folders, and pink for the third 1,000 folders, to prevent or reduce misfiling.

Colored labels may be used in the same way as colored folders. If your office orders a large quantity of standard folders and you cannot change the color, the label will allow for flexibility to meet your needs.

Color bar systems are available commercially from several manufacturers including Kardex Systems, Inc.; SFI Codacolor Filing Systems; Smead Manufacturing Company, and Visible Record Equipment Company. Although each of these systems has different features from the others, the basic concept is the use of one or more color bar labels attached to each folder or blocked out with a marker on a preprinted folder tab so that the total number of folders is divided into distinctly marked groups of ten to twenty folders by these "color bands." Usually color-coded files are stored on open shelves so that the file worker looking for a particular color group can scan many files at once. When replacing a folder having a red band above a blue band on the tab, scanning the shelves for similar color combinations is faster than looking for the letters of each unit.

In many color systems folders are not filed alphabetically within their group; instead, they are placed at the front of the group since 80 percent of the filing activity is normally concentrated in 20 percent of the records.

Thus the chances are 8 out of 10 that the search for a file will be limited to the front 20 percent of the color section. A color system can be used for straight numeric, middle digit, or terminal digit as well as for alphabetic filing systems.

MICROGRAPHICS

Micrographics is a term used for the process of reproducing information on microforms. A *microform* is either film or paper which contains microimages. A *microimage* is a reduction of a larger record or document. *Microfilm* is a roll of attached microimages. *Microfiche* is a sheet of film which contains a great many pages in miniature. The sheet is usually 6 by 4 inches and holds from 60 to 100 pages of records, depending on the reduction. An *aperture card* is a card with an opening, or aperture, in which microfilm is mounted. The microfilm image is usually a great reduction of a large document, such as an engineering drawing. Identifying data is usually printed on the card. Compared with other microforms, aperture cards have limited use.

ADVANTAGES OF MICROFILM. Microfilm is used for storing information and records because:

1. It provides a rapid way to locate information: information is located automatically on a machine called a *reader*. Locating a paper in traditional files takes much longer.
2. Microfilm is small and requires less storage space than paper records in cabinet files. Because of this, an operator can have many rolls of microfilm at the work station.
3. Microfilm readers are usually equipped to print copies of the records being located. Thus the operator can find and print the copy in one operation.
4. Microfilm is neater and cleaner than files, particularly those containing carbon copies of materials.
5. Microfilm stores a series of records on one piece of film; thus it is impossible to misplace an individual record.
6. Microfilm can be used for storing graphic data (pictures and drawings) as well as alphanumeric data.
7. Microfilm results in a permanent tangible record which can be read directly as opposed to computer tapes and word processing media which cannot.
8. Microfilm can be easily transported to be read wherever a reader is available, including at home with a portable reader. Readers are relatively small compared with other types of office equipment.
9. Conversion to microfilm is generally easier than conversion of the same data to computerized files. The hard-copy records can be photographed and the film developed either in-house or by an outside agency for use within a relatively short period of time. Developing

A TYPICAL MICROFILMING OPERATION

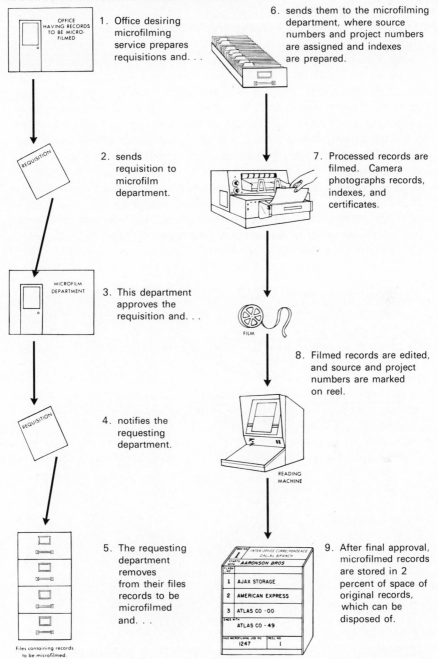

1. Office desiring microfilming service prepares requisitions and. . .

6. sends them to the microfilming department, where source numbers and project numbers are assigned and indexes are prepared.

2. sends requisition to microfilm department.

7. Processed records are filmed. Camera photographs records, indexes, and certificates.

3. This department approves the requisition and. . .

8. Filmed records are edited, and source and project numbers are marked on reel.

4. notifies the requesting department.

5. The requesting department removes from their files records to be microfilmed and. . .

9. After final approval, microfilmed records are stored in 2 percent of space of original records, which can be disposed of.

the indexing system is the most complicated part of the implementation of microfilm as a storage medium.

10. Microfilm costs less to mail than paper copies of the same number of pages. This results in a considerable cost savings for business.

Microfilming is used more and more in business for these reasons:

1. The cost of microfilm is decreasing and the equipment is available in a competetive market. As the cost of maintaining traditional filing systems increases, business will consider microforms to reduce space and labor costs.
2. The federal government will now allow microfilm records to be substituted for original documents; however, the film must not have been spliced. (Some records must be filmed in exact sequence to meet legal requirements. If a record is found to be out of sequence, the entire roll of film must be redone.)
3. New equipment is producing better images, so that it is easier to read the screens and to read the copies being produced.
4. Indexes may be prepared by file workers before or after the microfilming takes place. For some applications, indexes may be automatically prepared by a computer. (An accurate index is vital; without it records cannot be located once they have been filmed.)

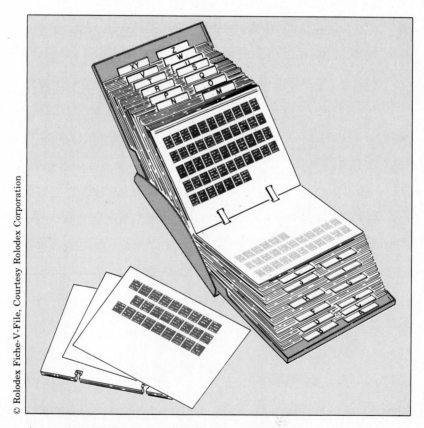

© Rolodex Fiche-V-File, Courtesy Rolodex Corporation

A binder holds plastic sleeves containing microfiche. The sheets of microfiche are easy to locate and are protected from scratches and smudges.

ADVANTAGES OF MICROFICHE. Microfiche has many of the same advantages as microfilm. In addition:

1. A sheet of microfiche is easier to use than a roll of film because you can immediately access the particular item or page you need instead of scanning a whole roll of film. Microfiche is set up with an alphanumeric matrix. Columns and rows are labeled so that if you need an item in Column B, Row 4, for example, you can immediately access that location.
2. Microfiche can be updated by adding pages. Additions, however, may cause pages to be out of sequence, which may destroy the legal value of the film.
3. Images can be deleted by photocopying over the image several times to black it out and make it unreadable. Microfiche can also be duplicated for use by others with some of the images omitted.

DISADVANTAGES OF MICROFILM AND MICROFICHE. Several disadvantages of using microfilm and microfiche for records storage are:

1. Paper copies from microfilm and microfiche are slow and expensive to produce and are of poor quality compared with other copying methods.
2. Microfilm is difficult to update since a new document cannot be inserted in place of an old one without destroying the integrity of the film by splicing it. Documents can be added to microfiche only in blank spaces; old documents cannot be replaced with new ones.
3. Special equipment is needed to read documents on microfilm and microfiche.
4. It is not possible to write on microfilm and microfiche in order to make notations or highlight information. It is also difficult to write on the copies that are produced.

Offices use micrographics for records storage; microfiche and microfilm readers are set up near the storage area for records. Portable readers enclosed in attaché cases extend the convenience of microforms. Businesses which print large documents that employees must take to other locations often use microforms to reduce the volume.

OTHER MICRO USES. The value of micrographics extends beyond its use in records management. *Micrographics* applies to the production of records for public use. *Micropublishing* is the production of information on microforms. *Microrepublishing* is the reproduction of information, previously in hard-copy form, on microforms.

Microfacsimile is the transmission of data contained on microfiche or aperture cards over telephone lines to produce hard copy at the other end. This is similar to *facsimile,* the transmission of hard copy from one location to another over telephone lines.

CAR AND COM. You are likely to hear the term *CAR* if you work in an office which has a computer to store and process information. CAR means "computer assisted retrieval" and refers to records which are stored within the computer on magnetic tapes or discs. You need the computer to obtain the desired information and produce it for you in readable form.

One of the advantages of CAR is that large quantities of information can be stored in a computer and the person requesting information can ask for it under different topics, to check all possibilities. There are storage banks of up-to-date information on topics included in books, articles, and documents. An individual seeking information queries the system to find out what is available about a particular topic. For example, a doctor may seek information about the causes and cures of a rare disease contracted by a patient.

OFF-LINE COM OPERATION

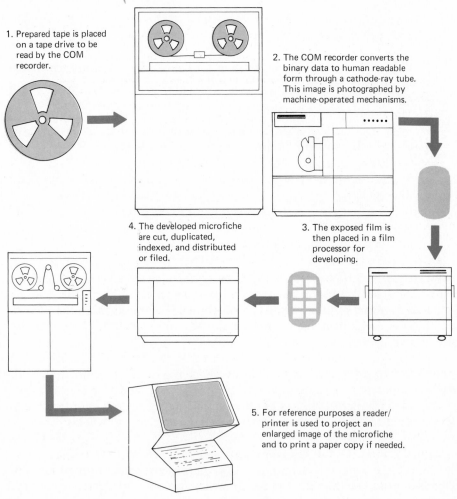

1. Prepared tape is placed on a tape drive to be read by the COM recorder.

2. The COM recorder converts the binary data to human readable form through a cathode-ray tube. This image is photographed by machine-operated mechanisms.

4. The developed microfiche are cut, duplicated, indexed, and distributed or filed.

3. The exposed film is then placed in a film processor for developing.

5. For reference purposes a reader/ printer is used to project an enlarged image of the microfiche and to print a paper copy if needed.

1.
Completed census forms
from 275,000 districts
arrive in boxes at three
census processing centers
in Jeffersonville, Ind., New
Orleans, or Laguna Niguel,
Calif.

2.
One-page forms are copied on microfilm at the rate of 130
pages per minute. For multiple-page forms, a brush turns and
flattens each page before it is photographed.

3.
The forms themselves are shredded after the film is processed.

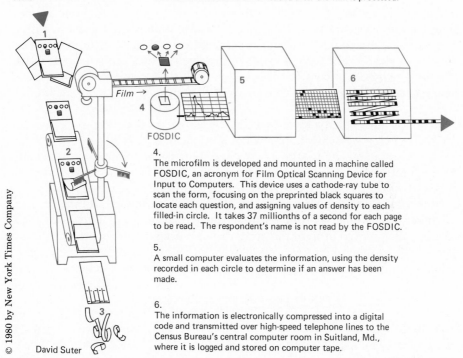

© 1980 by New York Times Company

David Suter

4.
The microfilm is developed and mounted in a machine called
FOSDIC, an acronym for Film Optical Scanning Device for
Input to Computers. This device uses a cathode-ray tube to
scan the form, focusing on the preprinted black squares to
locate each question, and assigning values of density to each
filled-in circle. It takes 37 millionths of a second for each page
to be read. The respondent's name is not read by the FOSDIC.

5.
A small computer evaluates the information, using the density
recorded in each circle to determine if an answer has been
made.

6.
The information is electronically compressed into a digital
code and transmitted over high-speed telephone lines to the
Census Bureau's central computer room in Suitland, Md.,
where it is logged and stored on computer tape.

COM refers to "computer output microfilm" or "computer output microfiche." Most computers have the capability to print information in hard
copy. COM allows information to be printed on microforms for use and
storage. The computer processes the desired information into a form readable by the microform processing unit, and that unit produces the microform
desired by the user.

A recent development is word processing on microfilm (WPOM), which
converts information on word processing magnetic media to microfilm for
storage and use.

It is predicted that the use of micrographics will continue to increase in
the office. The use of microforms to store documents is expected to grow
rapidly, particularly in those organizations that already have installed
complex computer and word processing systems. It is becoming economically feasible to add capabilities to already established equipment and
transmit data electronically via microfilm to another location.

EQUIPMENT AND STORAGE FOR MICROFORMS AND MAGNETIC MEDIA.   Today, with the rapid growth in the use of microforms and magnetic media used with word processing equipment, office supply manufacturers are developing compact files to use for efficient storage of these items. This equipment is usually of the drawer or tub type. A cabinet with drawers sized to fit microfilm or microfiche can hold many times the number of records compared to a standard vertical correspondence file of similar dimensions.

Because misfiling is a major problem with film records, only one person should do the actual storage. Records are coded numerically to make filing and expansion easy. An index is consulted to obtain the number of the desired record. Since these records are highly organized, this index is often stored on magnetic media or accessed by means of a computer for updating and producing a new copy. One piece of film may be the index for many others.

Magnetic media may be filed in a standard folder within a cardboard protective jacket attached to the folder, along with a hard (paper) copy of the material stored on the media. The hard copy may have a number typed on it which refers to the number printed on the card or disk where the material is stored. This is useful in locating the media when revisions are made or original copies are duplicated. Floppy disks may be filed in albums similar to those which hold 45-rpm records (illustrated on page 157). Tub files which can be moved around the office are also used for storing floppy disks. The disks are placed in hanging folders within the tub. Small racks containing hanging folders may be used on desk tops for easy access.

AUTOMATED FILING UNITS

It is possible to purchase automated filing units of various levels of sophistication. One company manufactures a system for microfiche which, when the index number is keyed in, will search the files and the materials contained in a special unit waiting to be filed and bring the jacket containing one or more microfiches out of the system for the user. Minitrieve, manufactured by Supreme Equipment and Systems Corp., uses a four-digit number entered on a keyboard to retrieve from two vertical banks of metal files the desired container and bring it by means of a cantilever shelf to the work station. When the filing is finished, the "restore" button is pushed and the file is returned to its proper location. This system may hold computer tapes, cards, or folders. Generally automated systems have the following advantages:

1. They can be locked for security.
2. They are more convenient and comfortable to use than conventional systems. The operator sits at a work station and files are brought there.
3. They save space by using vertical space rather than additional floor space.
4. They allow individuals with physical handicaps to work with the files.

Where a great many microfiche records must be stored, using automatic equipment that permits instant retrieval increases efficiency.

5. They are more attractive than conventional file cabinets and fit in with the open office setting.

TOTAL OFFICE AUTOMATION, OR THE PAPERLESS OFFICE

The term *paperless office* refers to those organizations that change correspondence and other business records into electronic and/or micrographic media in order to carry on everyday business activities. The collection, compilation, computation, and distribution of information can be handled by the use of large-scale computer networks. With the employment of sophisticated text-editing software, users can have at their fingertips, via a small computer, access to all the files and other information pertaining to the company's business.

The user can generate reports, update and edit reports, eliminate extraneous or unwanted information, cause information pertinent to the report to be edited, and cause this information to be returned to the computer for future reference or printing. Most text-editing systems require authority (that is, terminal identification, sign-on signatures, and so on) to limit access to persons who have authority to make these changes. The printing can take place in the computer room, or the information can be transmitted to another computer thousands of miles away and be printed there.

ADVANTAGES OF A PAPERLESS SYSTEM.   The source documents for business information, instead of being paper, are actually the electronic storage media in the computer. The advantages of a system such as this include:

1. Reduced cost through less consumption of paper.
2. Immediate access to information.
3. Elimination of the problems of misfiling and lost records.
4. Improved security of records since they are protected through the authority routines required to gain access to the information.
5. Significantly reduced physical storage space.
6. Easy interchange of necessary information between distant points.

OFFICE ENVIRONMENT AND SYSTEM DESIGN.   With office automation that eliminates paper records, a number of items can be totally removed from the office scene. Such things as the desk, calendar, in and out boxes, tickler files, calculator, travel expense vouchers, personal files, office copiers, card files, telephone logs, spelling dictionaries, clocks, personal diaries, and many other items which are a routine part of the executive's day can be eliminated. The standard office typewriter would not be necessary in an automated office. However, it is significant to note that *keyboarding skills are of extreme importance in such an office environment.* It is through keyboarding that all information is collected, compiled, computed, and distributed. The pencil and pencil sharpener are as unnecessary as paper in such an office. Even the executive will use keyboarding skills to access the computer for input and output.

A good example of the elimination of paper in various systems would be the airline ticket desk. You can call a travel agent or an airline and acquire reservations on a flight. Your reservation is recorded by the personnel in the travel agency or the airline office. No paper is generated until you arrive at the ticket desk at the airport. At that time, the clerk in charge accesses the computer by using keyboarding skills to locate your reservation and tells the computer to print your ticket.

Because these systems are designed by humans, system architecture is developed through processes we understand and know. Hence an understanding of manual filing and data management systems is extremely valuable inasmuch as it allows the user to know what the computer is doing with the information it maintains. The system handles the data in the same way you would manage a manual system. Needless to say, the system works at an extremely high rate of speed, making it much more efficient. (Some systems are able to read 8 million characters per second!)

MOBILITY.   In the past, the user has been restricted to the confines of an office because of the necessity of having files on paper readily available for use. In a paperless office, the user is limited only to the availability of a telephone. The use of portable terminals enables the user to feed and retrieve information from the system while at home, at field sites, in customers' offices, in hotels thousands of miles away, or with a mobile telephone while driving to and from work.

Courtesy Micronet, Incorporated and A. B. Dick

The "paperless" office may include an installation with an updatable microfiche camera and related equipment. In this office the camera is located in the cabinet that is at the bottom left. Above it is the platen where documents are placed for filming. Camera controls are on the panel, bottom right, and a microfiche reader is on the counter above the panel. At the top left is a binder with panels of microfiche, and to the right of the reader is a grid used to determine the frame for updating microfiche images.

ELECTRONIC MAIL.   One of the more common means of receiving input in an office that has not been automated is the postal system—the *mail*. With the paperless office, electronic mail is the key term.

Organizations large and small have a definite and growing requirement for electronic mail—now and in the coming years. Given today's fast-paced lifestyle, documents must be in the hands of individuals thousands of miles apart, simultaneously. Through the use of computers and telephone lines, documents can be transmitted at high rates of speed as simply and easily as making a phone call from one individual to another. Electronic mail creates many opportunities for companies to reduce costs. It also creates business opportunities for companies offering new products and services related to electronic mail.

WHAT WILL THIS OFFICE LOOK LIKE?   The decor of the office of the future will change to allow a less-structured and more relaxed, thought-provoking atmosphere. Desks, filing cabinets, and the like will disappear to be replaced by a living-room decor. This environment will allow the user to spend time valuably in original thought processes as opposed to manual filing, retrieving, and data management. Hence there will be more administrative power for more people.

Remember, the computer is only a tool to be used by people—but what a marvelous tool indeed!

FROM VOICE TO WRITTEN WORD.   In the future, as these systems become more sophisticated, data management and manipulation—both input and output—will be accomplished through the human voice. For example, the user will be able to pick up a phone and talk to the computer directly in plain English. The machine and the user will be able to converse about what the user desires and requires, and the user will direct the computer to provide the user's needs. Also, the computer will provide preprogrammed information, such as a reminder of a meeting or important reports due, birthdays, anniversaries, weather, news, and so on, by the spoken word. In much the same way, your telephone system can provide directory assistance to you via computer and the human voice.

LASER THUMBPRINT SCANNER AND VOICE ANALYZERS.   Among other innovations to aid in the creation of a paperless office and society are such devices as the laser thumbprint scanner and voice analyzers which substitute for signatures (as signatures can be easily forged). These also can be used as a key to provide access to computer information.

Whereas you now go to a gasoline station and sign a ticket to charge your gasoline, in the future you will be able to verify the data the operator has entered on a computer and signify your approval by thumbprint or voice.

It is significant to note that the computer and the system are simply tools as the saw is a tool to a carpenter. This tool is indeed not the answer to all problems; however, it is a tool that can be used to our advantage. Anyone who works in an office needs to know the basics of filing—that is, indexing rules, procedures, and basic elements of manual filing systems—in order to be able to understand and fully utilize the computer as a tool.

JOB ADVANCEMENT.   Job advancement will be determined by the employee's knowledge of basics. In order to advance in the automated office, it is *imperative* that you know the basics. Otherwise, you will only be able to do tomorrow what you have done today. Many people believe that it is possible to avoid learning these basics—that they can "let the computer do it." These people will not advance without a solid background of fundamentals that will allow them to fully utilize all the tools available to them.

SURVEY OF COMPETENCIES

GENERAL REVIEW

The following questions will help you to reinforce your learning of the competencies included in this chapter.

1. What are the four major developments in specialized systems being used in filing and records management?   (Competency 1)

2. Why are color systems used? How do these differ from what you learned about alphabetic and number systems previously in this book? (Competencies 2, 3)
3. Define the following terms:

aperture cards	microform
CAR	micrographics
COM	microimages
microfacsimile	micropublishing
microfiche	microrepublishing
microfilm	
(Competency 4)	

4. What is the difference between microfilm and microfiche? What are the advantages and disadvantages? (Competency 5)
5. What are the steps in the microfilming process? (Competency 5)
6. What are the advantages of automated filing units? (Competency 6)
7. List the advantages of a paperless office. (Competency 7)
8. Explain why a knowledge of filing basics is extremely important when working with computers. (Competency 8)
9. List some of the traditional items of records management equipment that will not appear in the office of the future. (Competency 9)

CASE PROBLEMS

1. A friend, Adam Chamberlain, says that misfiling is the biggest problem in his office. His employer wants him to find a way to avoid this problem, but he doesn't know where to begin. What advice can you give him? (Competencies 2, 3)
2. You overheard two office workers recently discussing filing in their offices. One individual said that nothing new has been going on in the area of filing; the other took the opposite point of view. Which individual is right? Would that necessarily apply to all offices? (Competencies 1, 2, 3, 4, 5, 6, 7, 9)
3. Your boss has told you that many of the records in your office are going to be placed on microfilm. Several of your co-workers are opposed to this idea. Can you tell them any advantages of microfilming for your office? (Competency 5)

If you have not mastered all of the competencies reviewed in the Survey, reread that part of the chapter which deals with the competency in question; then recheck your progress.

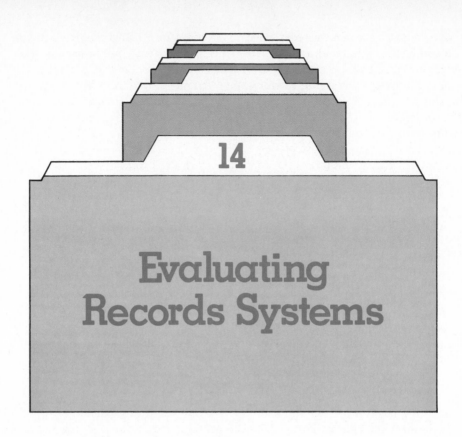

14

Evaluating
Records Systems

When you have completed this chapter, you will be able to:

1. Define *activity ratio* and *accuracy ratio,* and state how each can be improved.
2. State at least three questions that should be considered in evaluating equipment.
3. State at least four questions that should be considered in evaluating supplies.
4. List ten questions employees in a small organization might ask about their filing system to check its efficiency.
5. State three activities included in forms analysis, and give examples when forms are useful.
6. State factors to consider in the construction and layout of a form and why these factors are important.
7. Construct a form that meets the criteria for efficient design.

EVALUATING RECORDS SYSTEMS

Efficient records management requires periodic checkups on filing systems, procedures, office forms, and methods used by employees. Can records be obtained promptly and economically? Are office forms designed to provide information readily and accurately? Is the present equipment serving the system efficiently? Questions such as these must be considered periodically.

A large firm with centralized files may keep a record of the filing activity in the organization through daily, weekly, or monthly volume reports. These reports show the total number of records filed, the number of records requested from the files, and the number found and not found. The evaluation is made either by comparing present performance with past performance or by determining the activity ratio or the accuracy ratio. This information is useful in evaluating the effectiveness of the filing system.

ACTIVITY RATIO. The activity ratio, or percentage of filed records requested, lets the file worker or supervisor know whether too many records are being kept in the active files. The formula for the ratio is:

$$\frac{\text{Request for records}}{\text{Number of records in active files}} = \text{Activity ratio}$$

If 20,000 records are in the files and 5,000 are requested from them during a filing period, the activity ratio for that period is:

$$\frac{5,000}{20,000} = 25\% \text{ activity ratio}$$

If the activity ratio is higher than 20 percent, it is more than likely that the files do not contain too many unnecessary records. If the ratio is between 10 and 20 percent, some of the records in the active files probably should be transferred. An activity ratio below 10 percent means that many records in the active files should be transferred to storage.

ACCURACY RATIO. The accuracy ratio, or percentage of requested records found, is a good indication of the efficiency of both the filing system and employee work routines. The formula is as follows:

$$\frac{\text{Records found}}{\text{Records requested}} = \text{Accuracy ratio}$$

If 3,000 records are requested and 2,940 are found during a filing period, the accuracy ratio for that period is:

$$\frac{2,940}{3,000} = 98\% \text{ accuracy ratio}$$

If the accuracy ratio is higher than 99.5 percent, filing can be considered very efficient. A ratio under 97 percent is an indication that attention should be given to one or more of the following: indexing and coding, cross-referencing, storing procedures, charge-out and follow-up procedures, and checking on unnecessary retention of records in employees' desks.

EVALUATING FILING EQUIPMENT AND SUPPLIES

Evaluation of filing efficiency must also include a systematic study of file equipment and supplies. Have the right tools been selected to do the job? Since the biggest expenses are the salaries of the employees who work with the files, any changes or modifications in the equipment and supplies that will save workers' time will save money for the business.

EVALUATING EQUIPMENT. The evaluation of file equipment requires careful thought and consideration.

1. Is the equipment in good condition? If not, what repairs need to be made? Would the cost of new equipment be offset by an increase in worker performance?
2. Is the equipment arranged for efficient use? Does the layout need to be replanned to increase worker performance? Is there enough aisle space?
3. Can files be located more conveniently and serve double duty, that is, as counters, credenzas, or dividers in a landscaped office?
4. Would a change in equipment, particularly from file drawers to open-shelf filing, allow more efficient use of space and easier access? (See Chapter 10.)
5. Is proper storage equipment used for various types of records? Cards, magnetic tapes, cassettes, floppy disks, computer printouts, blueprints, and so on, have special storage requirements. Are the facilities available being used properly or does new equipment need to be provided for keeping items other than standard file folders stored efficiently? (See Chapter 10.)

EVALUATING SUPPLIES. The kinds of supplies used should be surveyed and analyzed periodically to ascertain whether or not they are doing their job.

1. Are the proper number of guides being used in each file drawer or on each shelf? The number of file guides in each drawer—usually between twenty and forty—will provide proper distribution of records, make reference to the files easy, and furnish support for the folders.
2. Are the supplies durable enough for the job? Are the least expensive supplies being used for items which are stored only for short periods or updated frequently?
3. Would laminating or some other means of protecting records save redoing the original from time to time?
4. Are the supplies being used readily available from suppliers? Can quantities needed be planned enough in advance to obtain discounts or take advantage of special offers?

5. Are the out guides and carrier folders or other supplies used for transporting or replacing records the right size and type?
6. Would it be more efficient to make copies of some items rather than remove the original and then have to return it to the file?
7. Can any of the supplies be sold for recycling after they are no longer usable or needed?

EVALUATING THE FILE SYSTEM OF A SMALL ORGANIZATION

Large organizations usually employ records managers or hire outside consultants to evaluate their filing systems, but small organizations often do not take the time to do a thorough evaluation of equipment and supplies. However, evaluation is important whatever the size of the organization. A group of individuals in the office may form a committee to study the files and supplies and make suggestions and recommendations for improvements. The list of questions which follows may be helpful:

1. Is the filing system proper for the function the records have?
2. Are the records given the required protection against fire, theft, and dampness?
3. Are records filed daily or more often if necessary?
4. Are important records being "filed" in desk drawers or trays?
5. Are useless materials being filed?
6. Are there many instances of misfiled or lost records?
7. Are there new developments in equipment or supplies that will improve operations?
8. Are file drawers overcrowded?
9. Is there an adequate number of guides (at least twenty) for each drawer?
10. Is an individual folder prepared when five or more papers accumulate from one correspondent?
11. Is the number of papers in any standard folder limited to a maximum of 100?
12. When papers need fastening within a folder, are staples rather than paper clips used?
13. Do the file drawers, guides, and folders bear descriptive labels and captions?
14. Are standard indexing rules used?
15. Is there adequate cross-referencing?
16. Are the records properly coded?
17. Are the records sorted in the best way before storing?
18. Is there a charge-out and follow-up system that is used properly by all employees?
19. Is there adequate provision for transfer and disposal?
20. Is there a manual that describes the filing operations of the business?

If these twenty checklist questions are answered and the shortcomings they reveal corrected once during each filing period (just before transfer time), files are likely to remain in efficient working condition. Even in the one-employee office, frequent attention to such a list can mean the difference between a neat, businesslike atmosphere and a desk full of disorganized papers.

A small office will be able to get help from the vendors of filing equipment and supplies. Since representatives of the vendors are employed to sell their particular products, you should be aware of their biases. However, if you seek information about the products of two or three different companies, you can compare the services and equipment they offer and make some decisions about what will work best for you. Salespeople who know the products of several companies will sometimes make suggestions about a competitor's product that would fit your particular need if the product you seek is not made by the salesperson's own company. These individuals try to satisfy the customer in the hope of making more sales in the future.

FORMS ANALYSIS

Printed forms are the most efficient carriers of business data, so they are the record most frequently used in offices. Writing a letter to order supplies, for example, is not nearly as efficient as using a printed form. It takes more time to compose and type a letter; it is harder for the departments that need to process the information or for the vendor to locate the essential information in a letter; it is not as convenient to circulate a letter as it is a printed form with multiple copies labeled for routing. A letter also is apt to omit essential information or to provide unnecessary information and thereby cause delay or error in completing the order.

If a form is not well designed, however, it may not serve its purpose well. For this reason, forms analysis is an important function; it should be carried out at regular intervals to see whether the office forms that are being used are doing their job. Forms analysis includes (1) the evaluation of individual forms to determine how they relate to other forms and how they affect the flow of work in the organization, (2) the improvement of old forms, and (3) the design of new forms.

EVALUATING EXISTING FORMS. When repetitive information is required—such as date, invoice number, name and address—and when these facts must be organized for fast processing, forms are extremely useful. Records managers do not recommend using a form unless there is a definite need because it is expensive to purchase or to design and print a form. A business form is not needed and should be eliminated if (1) the information it calls for is not used; (2) another source for the information is available; or (3) the cost of the form (largely the labor cost of filing it) exceeds its value. When forms are being evaluated, the question "How will this information be used?" should be asked for each item.

The question of whether or not multiple copies are needed should also be investigated. Multiple-copy carbon packs or packs with chemically treated

ROUTING MULTIPLE COPIES

In some large organizations, records are
prepared in multiple copies so that
different departments may have their own
copies. Notice that the same record is
stored in three different ways, according
to how it will be requested.

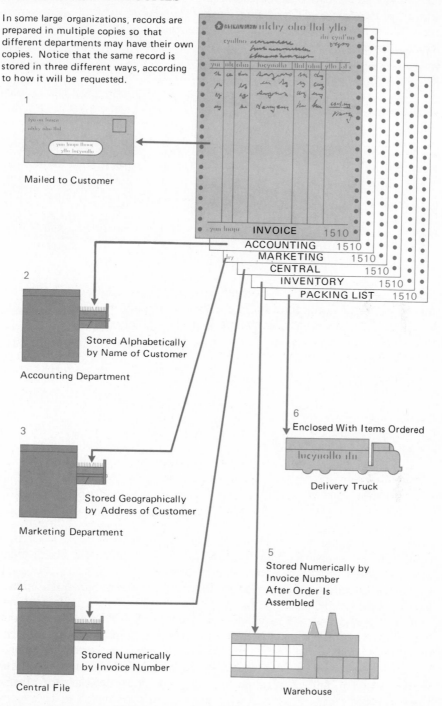

1

Mailed to Customer

2

Stored Alphabetically
by Name of Customer

Accounting Department

3

Stored Geographically
by Address of Customer

Marketing Department

4

Stored Numerically
by Invoice Number

Central File

5

Stored Numerically by
Invoice Number
After Order Is
Assembled

Warehouse

6

Enclosed With Items Ordered

Delivery Truck

INVOICE 1510
ACCOUNTING 1510
MARKETING 1510
CENTRAL 1510
INVENTORY 1510
PACKING LIST 1510

paper are expensive. If they are not needed or do not serve their intended
purpose, they should be eliminated. Besides the cost of the multiple-copy

form itself, unneeded extra copies result in (1) loss of employee time in handling, reading, and filing copies and (2) waste of valuable filing space.

REVISING EXISTING FORMS. Forms analysis may suggest ways to improve the design of the office forms in use, such as combining several forms into one, eliminating one or more copies, adding copies, splitting one form into two or more new ones, or eliminating certain forms. The analysis may also reveal the need for additional forms to improve the work flow in the office.

PURCHASING NEW FORMS. Standard forms are available at office supply stores. Telephone information pads, purchase requisitions, invoices, receipts, statements, journals, ledgers, and other accounting forms are available. Purchasing forms on the market of course is less costly for a business than designing and creating its own forms, but the forms analyst or office worker should be careful that the standard forms meet the needs of the office.

FORMS DESIGN

When plans for the design of a new form are made, the important part a form plays in the functioning of the firm becomes clear. The following paragraphs explain some of the considerations that enter into the design.

CONSTRUCTION. Construction of the form has to do with its physical characteristics—whether multiple copies are needed, size and shape, and quality of paper.

Plan for Routing and Mailing. The designer of a form must take into consideration how it will be routed and dispatched to and from other departments or businesses. If the use of the form is restricted to the office, the routing information may be placed on the form itself, thereby eliminating routing slips or transmittal memorandums.

If the form should have multiple copies for processing information by different departments, how the multiple copies will be made must be decided. Should the form have carbon inserts or be on chemically treated paper to carry the impression? Papers of different colors may be used to signal which copies go where, or an identifying label may be printed at the bottom of the form.

Forms that are mailed to other organizations should be designed to speed the addressing, collating, folding, and inserting steps that the form must go through. For example, if window envelopes are to be used, the form should be designed so that the address can be seen through the window without unusual folding of the form. Since it is often necessary to encourage the return of forms, they can be designed with *self-mailers:* they can be printed on postcards or on sheets that can be folded and fastened and then used as envelopes.

Size. Forms requiring storage in other than standard-size filing cabinets can prove to be inefficient because of the extra cost of the equipment. Even legal-size cabinets cost more and occupy more space than standard letter-size ones. A small form can become hidden and difficult to find when filed with larger records. Likewise, a large form can take extra space and slow down file searching when it is folded to standard letter-size dimensions. Therefore, a form should usually be designed to have the same dimensions as the other records with which it will be stored.

Standard paper-mill sizes should also be considered before deciding on the size of a particular form. This will ensure minimum waste and lowest cost per form. The printer should be consulted for this information.

Properties of Paper. The amount and kind of handling the form will receive should be considered when selecting the type of paper. If forms are frequently removed from and reinserted in files, used for posting of additional data, or transported a great deal, they should be able to resist wear and tear.

Some of the properties of paper are weight, grade, and grain. When considering weight, the lightest paper that will give satisfactory results should be used. Of course, the heavier weights are more durable. Standard weights recommended for various records are as follows:

RECORD	RECOMMENDED WEIGHT
Legal documents	28-pound
Ledgers	24-pound
Letterheads or forms (single copy)	20-pound
1 to 4 copies of multiple forms	16-pound
5 to 8 copies of multiple forms	13-pound
9 or more copies of multiple forms	Tissue weight (or onionskin)

The grade of paper depends upon the ratio of fiber content to sulphite (wood pulp) content. The grade of paper recommended usually depends upon the life span of a form:

LIFE OF FORM	GRADE
1 to 5 years	100% sulphite
6 to 12 years	50% sulphite, 50% fiber
Over 12 years	100% fiber

Most paper, like wood, has grain characteristics. The grain should run up and down on a form that is posted by machine and stored vertically so that the form will remain upright and not curl in a vertical tub or tray.

LAYOUT. The layout of the information on the form requires decisions on the wording of the guide words and phrases for readability, spacing to be allowed for information to be filled in, and the arrangement of the items on the form.

Readability.   Readability is important because the purpose of a form is to provide accurate, readily accessible information that can be used to make correct business decisions. The persons filling in the form must understand it before they can give the desired information. Techniques that improve readability of a form include the following:

1. *Titles* should be short and should indicate the purpose of the form. The word *form, sheet,* or *record* in a title is usually unnecessary. Compare these titles:

   Example A: Inventory Card Record for Files
   Example B: Factory Supplies Inventory

   In Example A, three words are unnecessary: *Card, Record,* and *Files.* Furthermore, the title omits important information about the kind of inventory record it is.

2. *Captions* (or questions) should be adapted to the background of the user of the form, and they should make responses easy—leaving no doubt as to what information is wanted. Compare these:

Example A
  What is your name and address?
  What is your age?
  How tall are you?
  How much do you weigh?
  What color are your eyes?

Example B

PRINT FULL NAME	FIRST	MIDDLE		LAST	
PRINT STREET ADDRESS OR R. F. D. NO.					
PRINT CITY AND STATE					
MONTH BORN	YEAR BORN	HEIGHT FT. IN.		WEIGHT	COLOR OF EYES

In Example B each item is blocked off for ease of reading and correct placement of data, and there is no doubt about what information

LONDON CORPORATION SUBSIDIARY OF FROZEN PRODUCE COMPANY
WELLSBORO, PENNSYLVANIA 16901

RECEIVING
REPORT

R 12010

| RECEIVED FROM | ADDRESS | DATE RECEIVED / / |
| PURCHASED FROM | ADDRESS | PURCHASE ORDER NO. |

RECEIVED VIA EXPRESS ☐ P.P. ☐ FREIGHT ☐ TRUCK ☐ LOCAL ☐	TRANSPORTATION CHARGES $	PREPAID	COLLECT	PURCH. REQUISITION NO.
CAR INITIALS & NO. WAYBILL NO.	BILL OF LADING NO.	PACKING SLIP NO.	CHARGE NO.
DELIVER TO	ACCEPTED BY	RECEIVED BY

QUANTITY RECEIVED	QUANTITY ACCEPTED	QUANTITY REJECTED	DESCRIPTION

INSPECTION RECORD

| RETURN TO VENDOR | REWORK | ACCEPTED | INSPECTOR'S SIGNATURE | DATE INSPECTED |
| REASON FOR REJECTION | | | | |

F-1003

This form combines several basic spacing designs, including captions (guide words) above the line of writing, boxes for checking responses, and a column arrangement to separate like information.

should be given. Before a form is printed, readability should be tested by having potential users fill in sample copies.

3. Most forms require accompanying *instructions*. When they are brief, such as "Print full name" in the example on page 184, they may be on the form itself. When they are lengthy or complex, instructions should be printed on the back of the form or in a separate manual that includes a filled-in sample illustration of the form.

Spacing. Forms filled in by hand should have writing spaces at least ¼ inch high for desk work and ⅓ inch high for field work, such as surveying or delivering. Horizontal space should be adequate for the information to be written in neatly.

For the design or improvement of forms to be typewritten, these facts about most standard typewriters must be considered: There are 6 vertical spaces per inch, there are 12 horizontal spaces per inch on elite-type machines and 10 on pica-type machines, and it is usually more efficient if the tabulator rather than the space bar can be used for moving from one item to another.

There are three basic spacing designs for forms that require handwritten or typewritten fill-ins:

1. Caption on or under the line of writing:

Ship via _____

_____
Ship via

2. Box design:

Ship via

3. Column arrangement:

			Ship via			

Each has its particular advantages or disadvantages. When captions are on the line of writing, the typist filling in the form must space through the printed words to reach the next typing position. Captions below the line are satisfactory for forms filled in by hand, but below-the-line captions are hidden on a typewriter. The box design, with captions printed in small type in the upper portion of the box, saves space and eliminates excessive typewriter spacing or adjustment. It also ensures correct placement of data. Column design facilitates the use of the typewriter tabulator. This design is especially useful when many numbers, such as prices of goods, are to be entered.

Sequence of Items. The sequence of items on a form should be determined by traditional reading habits, relation of the form to other forms, and frequency of use. People are accustomed to reading left to right, top to bottom. They are also used to seeing related items in a standard order, such as an address given first by house number, then by street, city, state, and ZIP Code. For fast processing of data, all items that are on related forms should be in the same sequence on all those forms. Items that are filled in on all the forms should be first; any that are not always filled in are placed at the right; those filled in on only a few of the forms should be at the bottom.

Boxes (commonly called *ballot boxes*) are used when a question may be answered *yes* or *no* or when a selection of answers can be listed. Contrast the following:

Example A | List the sports you are qualified to coach:

Example B

> Check the sports you are qualified to coach:
>
> ☐ football   ☐ baseball   ☐ soccer   ☐ other _____
>
> ☐ basketball   ☐ track   ☐ tennis   ☐ other _____

Sequence of items is important also for efficient filing. For example, an application form used at one time by a very large organization had the filing data—the applicant's name—in the center of the form. The forms were stored in vertical files. Clerks had to remove each form completely from the file and read the name, and this process had to be continued until the right application was reached. It took nine minutes, on the average, to find an application and only five minutes to process it. If the name had been on the upper edge of the form, instead of in the middle of the form, the correct application form could have been located in a fraction of a minute.

As the general rule, filing data on forms should be at the top when forms are filed vertically, at the visible edge when forms are filed in visible equipment, and at the side opposite the point of fastening when forms are bound. In making decisions as to placement of filing data, the following must be considered: In what type of equipment will the form be stored—standard file cabinet, open shelves, visible files, or other? Will the form be filed in folders or not? Will the form be fastened to other forms or papers? If so, where and with what type of fastener?

CONCLUSION

Now that you have reached the end of your study of filing systems and records management, take a moment to reflect on what you have learned. You found that filing may be a career. You learned rules for filing individual, business, and special names. You learned guidelines for managing correspondence, card records, and business forms. You learned how to file cards and correspondence numerically, geographically, and by subject. You learned procedures for records control and retention. You found that modern and sophisticated equipment and supplies are available to help you file and find efficiently. You learned how to set up your work station and how to set up a records system. You learned about several specialized systems which are available. In this last chapter you learned how to evaluate your system and how to develop forms to help make it work smoothly. Now you have a basic knowledge of filing and records management on which to build as you pursue a career in an office occupation. As you work with these concepts, you will be able to add to this knowledge and develop new and better ways to accomplish your job duties: you will consider filing and records management a part of your professional life.

SURVEY OF COMPETENCIES

GENERAL REVIEW

The following questions will help you to reinforce your learning of the competencies included in this chapter.

1. What is the activity ratio? What is the accuracy ratio? How can each be improved? (Competency 1)
2. How can file equipment and supplies be evaluated? (Competencies 2, 3)
3. What questions might employees in a small organization ask about their filing system to check its efficiency? (Competency 4)
4. What activities are included in forms analysis? (Competency 5)
5. When are forms useful? (Competency 5)
6. Give examples of changes that might be made after an evaluation of existing forms has been completed. How may existing forms be revised? When may standard forms be acceptable? (Competency 5)
7. Why are each of the following factors important in planning construction and layout of a form: routing and mailing, size, properties of paper, readability, spacing and sequence of items? (Competency 6)

CASE PROBLEMS

1. These two forms call for the same information, but they are designed differently. Which form would be easier to fill in? Which would give management more data? Can you suggest any improvements? (Competency 6)

VISUAL AIDS CORPORATION

Salesperson's Report of Exhibits

Booth No. _____ Dates _____

Stock Exhibited (List) _____

Number Registered _____ Number of Requests for Materials _____

Date _____ Signature of Salesperson _____

City and State _____ Name of Sponsoring Organization _____

The form here and the one at the top of the next page call for the same information, but they are designed differently. Which form would be easier to fill in? Which would give management more data?

VISUAL AIDS CORPORATION

Salesperson's Report of Exhibits at _____

City and State	Booth No.	Dates
Was Material Distributed? ☐ Yes ☐ No	If "Yes," Check Items Below	

Films _____	Visi-Guides _____
Records _____	Recorders _____
Filmstrips _____	Screens _____
Tapes _____	Projectors _____

Number Registered   Number of Requests for Materials

Date   Signature of Salesperson

2. Your instructor would like a form designed to collect information about the students in your filing and records management class. The following information should be included on the form: name; address; telephone number; date of birth; social security number or student identification number; courses being taken this quarter or semester; the name of your curriculum or major; the date you expect to graduate or complete the program; and the name, address, and telephone number of a relative to notify in the event of an emergency. Use this information to design an 8½- by 11-inch form to be placed in your student folder. Then use the information to design a 6 by 4 card to be placed in an office desk reference file.   (Competency 7)

3. Your friend Joe Mason has several complaints about the filing system in his office. The drawers are too crowded, and there does not seem to be enough space to put more cabinets in. His employer will consider purchasing new equipment, but Joe is not sure that will solve the problem. Much of the material currently being filed is printed on forms. Joe thinks some of these forms duplicate the information that is already on others. What advice can you give Joe?   (Competencies 1, 4, 5, 6)

4. You decide to evaluate how well you did in filing and finding items today. (a) You looked for 150 items and found 145 of them. What is your accuracy ratio? Is this sufficiently high? What questions should

you ask yourself to improve your ratio? **(b)** Suppose on another day 150 records were requested and you were able to find 148. What is your ratio on that day? Do you feel this ratio is acceptable? What ratio should you aim for? Do you feel that this ratio evaluates you as an employee? **(c)** Suppose you have 10,000 records on file and you use 150 different records each day. What is your activity ratio for 30 working days? Do you feel any unnecessary records are being kept on file? Do you feel you should be keeping more records than you are? **(d)** Suppose during this same 30-day filing period you had only 900 requests for records. What would be your activity ratio, and what would it indicate? (Competency 1)

5. You work in an office where you need to complete several different forms each day. You spend a great deal of time on some of the forms, while others are quick to fill in. As you study the forms, you find that it does not make any difference whether the forms are handwritten or typed, but it is the amount of information you need to write or type and the arrangement of the form that makes the work go faster on some forms. What characteristics of forms are found in the ones that are easy to do? (Competencies 4, 5, 6)

If you have not mastered all of the competencies reviewed in the Survey, reread that part of the chapter which deals with the competency in question; then recheck your progress.

Appendix

Following are sixteen exercises that apply the alphabetic indexing rules presented in Chapters 2 and 3. These exercises contain the same names as Jobs 1 to 16 in *Practice Materials for Filing Systems and Records Management, Third Edition.* Therefore, students who have the *Practice Materials* need not complete the following exercises.

Exercise 1

After studying Alphabetic Indexing Rules 1 to 3:

A.   Write each of the following names in correct indexing order on a separate 5 by 3 file card. The number before the name is to be placed in the upper right corner.

1. Melissa Rathbone
2. Curtiss Pittman
3. Albert S. Pittman
4. Walter P. Ragsdale
5. E. D. Pittman

6. Mildred Sager
7. B. Pittinger
8. S. M. Ratcliffe
9. A. Stephanie Pittman
10. Marvin Sagan

B.   Arrange the cards in correct alphabetic order.

C.   On an answer sheet similar to the one illustrated below, list the numbers on the file cards in the order in which they have been arranged. Hand in the answer sheet only.

Name *Student's Name*   Exercise No. ____*1*____

1. 7   6.
2. 9   7.
3. 3   8.
4.   9.
5.   10.

D.   Save the file cards for use in later exercises.

Exercise 2
After studying Alphabetic Indexing Rules 4 and 5:

A. Write each of the following names in correct indexing order on a separate 5 by 3 file card. The number before the name is to be placed in the upper right corner.

11. William M. Quinn
12. Eva St. Charles
13. Donald Tobin
14. Wilma St. George
15. A. Miranda Rathbone
16. Abel St. Cloud
17. Amanda Samuels
18. C. W. Pittman
19. E. St. Charles
20. Milton J. Ratliff

21. George-Anne Tolson
22. D. Tobin-Reynolds
23. G. Anne-Marie Tolson
24. A. Sagan
25. Dwight T. Reynolds
26. Robert J. Santacruz
27. Donald L. Tobin-Reynolds
28. Wilhamena Quinn
29. D. W. Rheynolds
30. I. F. Schrader

B. Follow the instructions for Exercise 1, saving the cards for use in later exercises.

Exercise 3
After studying Alphabetic Indexing Rules 6 to 8, prepare the file cards for the names below as instructed in Exercise 1. Follow those instructions to complete this exercise.

31. Isabelle F. Schrader
32. Willard J. Quigley
33. R. E. Rebovitch
34. Jas. L. Stallings
35. B. Pittenger, Sr.
36. Carl Schrader
37. Billy Staiman
38. Lorenzo Romano
39. Danny (Daniel P.) Tobin
40. R. Edward Rebovitch, Jr.

41. M. A. Small, Capt.
42. Muhammed Rahman
43. Thomasina Romero
44. B. H. Tobash
45. Geo. F. Smalley
46. Lorraine Romey
47. Jos. L. Stafford
48. Mrs. Mae Quidley
49. Merle A. Smallwood, M.D.
50. James R. Stallings, CPA

Exercise 4
For practice in applying Alphabetic Indexing Rules 1 to 8 and cross-referencing, follow the instructions below.

A. Arrange cards 1 to 50 in numeric sequence.

B. Prepare cross-reference cards similar to the one pictured near the top of page 193 for each of the following:

1. *Mildred Sager,* card 6; cross-reference under *Mildred Stallard,* card 6x.

2. *A. Stephanie Pittman,* card 9; cross-reference under *A. Stephanie Pittman-Abel,* card 9x.

3. *Wilhamena Quinn,* card 28; cross-reference under *Senator Quinn,* card 28x.

4. *Muhammed Rahman,* card 42; cross-reference under *Walter Taylor,* card 42x.

```
Stallard, Mildred                              6x

SEE:  Sager, Mildred
```

C. Arrange cards 1 to 50 and the four cross-reference cards alphabetically.

D. Fill in an answer sheet for Exercise 4. List the numbers of the cross-reference cards in addition to the numbers of the regular cards.

E. Save both the regular cards and cross-reference cards for future use.

Exercise 5

The goal of any filing system is *retrieval.* Speed in finding is essential to any office operation because time will be wasted if a record cannot be located. See how rapidly you can find the following cards from among those you alphabetized for Exercise 4. As you locate each card, write the information indicated on an answer sheet much like the one illustrated below.

R. Edward Rebovitch, Jr.
Donald Tobin
Eva St. Charles
Curtiss Pittman
D. W. Rheynolds

Lorraine Romey
Carl Schrader
Willard J. Quigley
M. A. Small, Capt.
Billy Staiman

Card No.	Name	Filed After Card No.	Filed Before Card No.
40	Rebovitch, R. Edward (Jr.)	33	25

Exercise 6

After studying Alphabetic Indexing Rules 9 and 10, prepare the file cards for the names below as instructed in Exercise 1. Follow those instructions to complete this exercise.

51. Sanders Store of Basics
52. The Rib Restaurant
53. Jose Perez
54. Savoy A. Schandelmeier
55. Research Services
56. Sanders Store for Boys
57. The Pet Farm
58. Peoples Insurance Services
59. Scally and Savoy, Incorporated
60. T. F. Pendergrass

Exercise 7

After studying Alphabetic Indexing Rules 11 to 14, prepare the file cards for the names below as instructed in Exercise 1. Follow those instructions to complete this exercise.

61. Southwest Medical Laboratory
62. Thompson's Steak & Seafood
63. Amanda Twyman
64. Rachel S. Smith
65. Amos W. Tweedy
66. Thomas Scalley
67. Toll House Restaurant
68. U L A Computer Services
69. Smith Transfer
70. Twin City Restaurant
71. Smile Realty
72. Tolentino's Pizza
73. U C Management Consultants
74. South West Apartments
75. Thomson's Paint Shop
76. Reginald W. Smith
77. John P. Scali
78. A. W. Tyndall
79. Emanuel Perry
80. Thomas Scanlan

Exercise 8

After studying Alphabetic Indexing Rules 15 to 18, prepare the file cards for the names below as instructed in Exercise 1. Follow those instructions to complete this exercise.

81. 21st Century Cinema
82. Pennell's Carryout
    425 N. Main Street
83. That's a Pizza
84. Penn's Flower Store
85. Temporary Help, Inc.
86. U-Rent Office Equipment
87. Printing by Perez
88. Wm. P. Pendergast
89. Twenty-Twenty Optical Services
90. Bertha A. Pendleton
91. Rent a Tool, Ltd.
92. Pennell's Carryout
    1721 Eastern Avenue
93. Phyllis A. Thatcher
94. Palm Springs Health Spas
95. 10 Office Plaza
96. Puerto Rico Millinery
97. Twenty-First Century Equipment
98. Pennell's Carryout
    119 N. Main Street
99. Twin Oaks Restaurant
100. U-Save Variety Shoppe

Exercise 9

For practice in applying Alphabetic Indexing Rules 1 to 18, arrange cards 51 to 100 in numeric sequence.

A.   Arrange the cards alphabetically.

B.   Fill in an answer sheet for Exercise 9.

C.   Save the cards for future use.

Exercise 10

See how rapidly you can find the following cards from among those you alphabetized in Exercise 9. As you locate each card, write on an answer sheet (see the illustration at the bottom of page 193) the information indicated in Exercise 5.

U-Save Variety Shoppe
A. W. Tyndall
Southwest Medical Laboratory
Penn's Flower Store
Toll House Restaurant

The Rib Restaurant
That's a Pizza
Savoy A. Schandelmeier
Twenty-Twenty Optical Services
Thomas Scalley

Exercise 11

After studying Alphabetic Indexing Rules 19 to 22, prepare the file cards for the names below as instructed in Exercise 1. Follow those instructions to complete this exercise.

101. Southeastern Louisiana State College
102. H. Seymour Reginald
103. Republic National Bank
104. St. Moritz Hotel
105. Peconic Bay General Hospital
106. Stephen L. Stratford
107. United Federal Bank
108. Regency Elementary School
109. Richmond Savings & Loan
110. The Hotel Regency
111. Richmond Public Library
112. Pablo Sainz
113. The Stratford Hotel
114. The Security National Bank
115. The Hotel Seagull
116. St. Monica's Medical Center
117. Standard Savings & Loan
118. Regis High School
119. Raceway Motel
120. Bruce Stratton
121. College of Stratford
122. The Travelers Hotel
123. Republic Memorial Hospital
124. R. St. Clair
125. United Family Clinic
126. University of Richmond
127. C. W. Traub
128. Stratford Theological Seminary
129. Patrick Travers
130. St. Michael's School of Music

Exercise 12

After studying Alphabetic Indexing Rules 23 to 25, prepare the file cards for the names below as instructed in Exercise 1. Follow those instructions to complete this exercise.

131. U.S. Air Force
132. Philadelphia Drug Treatment Services
133. Schaeffer County Treasurer's Office
134. Patricia J. Travenol, CPA
135. U.S. Environmental Protection Agency
136. Bonnie Stratton
137. Republic of Taiwan, Dept. of Agriculture
138. Antonio Sanchez
139. Textile Design Corporation
140. Thomas C. Schaffer
141. U.S. Administration on Aging
142. JoAnne Reiner
143. Equal Employment Opportunity Commission, U.S. Government
144. Texas Supreme Court
145. Richard's Anchor Repair
146. S. Frank Rafferty
147. U.S. District Court
148. Caroline O. Schaeffer
149. Alcohol, Tobacco, & Firearms Bureau, U.S. Government
150. Hayes W. Stratford

Exercise 13

For practice in applying Alphabetic Indexing Rules 1 to 25 and cross-referencing, follow the instructions below.

A. Arrange cards 101 to 150 in numeric sequence.

B. Prepare a cross-reference card for each of the following:

1. *Raceway Motel,* card 119; cross-reference under *Juanita Saunders, Manager,* card 119x.
2. *University of Richmond,* card 126; cross-reference under *University* (of) (first unit), *Richmond* (second unit), card 126x.
3. *Schaeffer County Treasurer's Office,* card 133; cross-reference under *Treasurer's Office* (first and second units), *Schaeffer County* (third and fourth units), card 133x.
4. *Texas Supreme Court,* card 144; under *Supreme Court* (first and second units), *Texas State* (third and fourth units), card 144x.

C. Arrange the cross-reference cards alphabetically with cards 101 to 150. Prepare an answer sheet for Exercise 13. List the numbers of the cross-reference cards in addition to the numbers of the regular cards. Save these cards for future use.

Exercise 14

See how rapidly you can find the following cards from among those you alphabetized in Exercise 13. As you locate each card, write on an answer

sheet (see the illustration at the bottom of page 193) the information indicated in Exercise 5 or 10.

The Hotel Seagull
U.S. District Court
Peconic Bay General Hospital
College of Stratford
Richard's Anchor Repair

Texas Supreme Court
Southeastern Louisiana State College
The Travelers Hotel
S. Frank Rafferty
Pablo Sainz

Exercise 15
This exercise may be used as additional filing practice or as a test. Your
instructor will indicate which.

A.   Prepare the file cards for the names below as instructed in Exercise 1.
     Follow those instructions to complete this exercise, including the cross-
     reference cards which are to be prepared according to the list following
     the names.

151. Sails of the Sea, Inc.
152. Peoples Hardware Inc.
153. E. P. Quick
154. R A P Enterprises
155. The Pepperoni Stick
156. Anna-Belle Retamozo
157. Ralph T. Scherer
158. The United Way Community
     Fund
159. Stevens' Discount City
     14 Furman Lane
160. Mrs. Thackery Thaler
161. Town & Country Furniture
     Co.
162. D. P. Snaith, M.D.
163. Walter Schiller-Smith
164. Ivan S. Peregonov
165. RBC Corporation
166. Mrs. Sarah Queen
167. Smithfield County, Consumer
     Protection Agency
168. Willie Robson
169. Rev. Wilbur Robottini
170. Victor F. Perez
171. Rob Ressler's Restaurant
172. Suzanne St. Paul
173. Stevens' Discount City
     219 Beverly Boulevard
174. Quality Steel Services

175. U.S. Management & Budget
     Office
176. David C. Stevenson
177. Turkey, Dept. of Labor
178. Perez Engineering Corp.
179. The Hotel Stevens
180. U.S. Marine Corps
181. Charlene E. Restaine
182. Franklin Q. Salerno
183. Retired Officers Hospital
184. Rev. Wilbur Rabinowitz
185. Tennessee, Division of Motor
     Vehicles
186. Samual O. Quam
187. Scher Rent a Tool
188. Smithfield National Bank
189. Quick Copy Printing, Ltd.
190. Hoai Than
191. Franklin P. Salerno
192. Mae-Ree Schell
193. Tots 'N Teens Wear, Ltd.
194. Robinson-Bryan Realty Co.
195. Rock Creek Nursing School
196. U.S. Maritime
     Administration
197. The Hotel Towers
198. Smith Storage Corp.
199. M. T. Rocha
200. 10-Ton Truck Repair

B. Prepare a cross-reference for each of the following:

1. *R A P Enterprises,* card 154; cross-reference under *Ryland, Asche, and Porter Enterprises,* card 154x.
2. *Quality Steel Services,* card 174; cross-reference under *Steel Services,* card 174x.
3. *Charlene E. Restaine,* card 181; cross-reference under *Charlene E. Underwood,* card 181x.
4. *Scher Rent a Tool,* card 187; cross-reference under *Rent a Tool,* card 187x.

Exercise 16

See how rapidly you can find the following cards from among those you alphabetized in Exercise 15. As you locate each card, record the information on an answer sheet such as the one at the bottom of page 193.

Samual O. Quam
Mrs. Thackery Thaler
Sails of the Sea, Inc.
The Pepperoni Stick
U.S. Maritime Administration

Turkey, Dept. of Labor
Anna-Belle Retamozo
The Hotel Stevens
Ralph T. Scherer
D. P. Snaith, M.D.

Glossary

Abbreviation A shortened form of a word. In indexing, an abbreviation is considered as though it were spelled out.

Accuracy ratio The percentage of requested records found during a filing period.

Acronym A word that has been constructed from initials or parts of other words, such as VISTA (Volunteers *in* Service *to* America).

Active file A filing cabinet reserved for records that are used frequently.

Activity ratio The percentage of filed records requested during a filing period.

Address file A card file containing frequently used names and addresses. Usually kept in a box or on a rotary wheel.

Alphabetic arrangement The listing of names or topics in sequence according to the alphabet. The process is called *alphabetizing.*

Alphabetic filing Any system in which the captions are names of people, organizations, or letters of the alphabet.

Alphabetic subject filing A filing system in which subject headings and divisions are alphabetized.

Alphabetize To arrange in sequence according to the letters of the alphabet.

AlphaZ Commercial color filing system.

Aperture cards Cards with a piece of microfilm mounted in an aperture to reduce part of a document, usually something quite large.

Archives The historical records kept by an organization.

ARMA Association of Records Managers and Administrators, Inc.

Auxiliary guide See *Secondary guide.*

Backshifting Shifting the location of records to allow for expansion at the beginning of a file.

Box files Low-cost steel or corrugated fiberboard files used for storage.

Business forms Papers or cards used in offices to record or process information of a repetitive nature in an efficient way.

CAR Computer-assisted retrieval.

COM Computer output microfilm.

Cabinet A container with one or more drawers or shelves for housing filed records.

Calendar pad A number of sheets of paper, usually twelve, that includes one for each month of the year, stacked and glued together at one end. Each sheet includes a box for each day of the month in which notations can be made regarding activities for that day.

Caption A name, letter, or number used to identify records for filing.

Card filing Processing and storing business information on cards. There are two kinds of card files—vertical and visible.

Card index A list that identifies assigned numbers in a numeric correspondence filing system.

Carousel files See *Rotary files.*

Carrier folder A folder, usually of a distinctive color and made of a strong material, that is used to transport records.

Centralized control A plan of organization whereby one person is responsible for all records management in the organization, whether files are centralized or decentralized.

Centralized files Files in which all records except highly specialized departmental ones are stored together.

Charge method A procedure used to account for records that have been removed from the files.

Charging out The procedure used to request and account for records removed from the files.

Chronological In sequence according to date. When records are filed chronologically, the latest date is usually in front.

Classifying Arranging in groups according to a predetermined plan.

Codacolor A commercial color filing system.

Coding The process of marking correspondence with the caption under which it will be stored.

Colorscan A commercial color filing system.

Combination subject file A method used when the volume of correspondence to be grouped by subject is small in comparison with records to be filed under the name of the person or organization. Subject captions are combined with name captions in one file.

Commercial system A set of ready-made guides and folders manufactured for immediate use.

Compound geographic name The name of a city, state, or other geographic location that includes more than one word.

Computer output microfilm Processing of information on magnetic tapes to microfilm or microfiche.

Computer-assisted retrieval A method of obtaining records stored within the computer or on magnetic tapes or disks processed by a computer.

Consecutive numeric system The most commonly used numeric system. In this system, numbers are used consecutively, or in order. For example, 101 precedes 102, which precedes 103.

Consultant One who gives professional advice, in this case concerning the operation and maintenance of files and records.

Contraction A shortened form of a word made by omitting letters and drawing the shortened form together. An example is *don't*.

Correspondence Any written communication that has not been designed to be placed in a card or forms file, such as letters, telegrams, orders, invoices, bills, checks, reports, and miscellaneous papers that are on sheets of paper and not on cards.

Correspondence book or correspondence file A chronological record of outgoing correspondence made by typing an extra carbon of correspondence and placing these carbon copies in a loose-leaf notebook with the most current document in front.

Cross-filing Filing a record under one or more additional captions under which it might also be requested or used. See *Cross-reference*.

Cross-indexing See *Cross-reference*.

Cross-reference A notation in a file or an index showing that the record being sought is stored elsewhere; or the filing of a duplicate of an original record in other locations where it might be sought.

Cut The size of the tab on the back flap of a folder, usually expressed in a fraction. *One-half cut,* for example, means that the tab takes up one-half of the back flap of a folder.

Cycle method See *Two-period transfer.*

Data filing See *Subject filing.*

Data processing A term coined by the computer industry that indicates a system in which information is used, produced, and maintained by electronic computers.

Date stamp A notation on an incoming piece of correspondence to indicate the date and, often, the hour of receipt.

Decentralized files See *Departmental files.*

Decentralized files with centralized control Departmental files kept according to regulations of a central authority in the organization.

Decimal-numeric system A numeric filing system used when headings are subdivided more than twice.

Degree An educational award, such as Doctor of Education (Ed.D.), that is conferred for certain advanced studies. Degree titles, such as Doctor, are not filing units when they precede the full name of an individual.

Departmental files Files in which records of one department are stored separately from records of other departments.

Desk trays Containers for incoming and outgoing correspondence kept on desks.

Desk-drawer file A large file drawer contained in a desk.

Dictionary arrangement Organization of a subject file with headings that do not have divisions or subdivisions.

Direct A filing system that permits the location of records without reference to an index.

Disposing, disposition Destroying or eliminating records that are no longer needed.

Document A paper containing information.

Double capacity See *Two-period transfer.*

Double (or closed) captions Captions that indicate not only where the section of the file starts but also where it ends.

Drawer The part of a file cabinet that contains records.

Duplex-numeric system A type of numeric filing system used when there are more than ten main headings or more than nine divisions or subdivisions under the same heading.

Electric Refers to the operation of automatic files and data processing machines by means of an electric motor.

Electronic Refers to machines that process data by means of electric current and a minimum of moving parts.

Encyclopedic arrangement Organization of a subject file with main headings, divisions, and subdivisions.

Equipment The cabinets, furniture, and miscellaneous devices used in handling and storing records.

Essential records All those records needed to carry on a business.

Expansion Any increase in the amount of equipment and supplies to make possible the storing of more records.

Expansion scores See *Scores.*

Facsimile The transmission of hard copy from one location to another over telephone lines.

File cards Cardboard slips that are used in both vertical and visible files.

File shelf A shelf that is attached to the front or the side of a file drawer to hold records during filing and finding operations.

File worker An employee whose specialized job is to inspect, index, code, sort, and store records and to remove them from the files when they are needed.

Files Containers for storing records—cabinets, open shelves, boxes, or any other type of housing.

Filing The process of classifying, arranging, and storing records so that they can be obtained quickly when needed.

Filing period The span of time during which records remain in the active files.

Filing system An arrangement of equipment and supplies to permit the storing of records according to a definite plan.

Fill-ins, fill-in information See *Variable information.*

Film-reading machine A machine used to view information that has been photographed on microfilm.

Finish The relative smoothness of the surface of a card.

Flowchart The diagram of an operation on paper, from its beginning to its end, so that all of its steps can be easily seen and evaluated.

Folder A manila or fiber container that holds correspondence in files.

Followers or compressors Movable supports that expand or contract the usable space within a file drawer.

Follow-up A system of checking on borrowed records to effect their return to the files.

Follow-up file A file that calls attention to either (1) charged-out records or (2) an office job that requires action on a certain date. It is usually arranged chronologically.

Follow-up folder A folder with dates along the top edge that can be clearly marked with a signal indicating when the records within the folder require action.

Forms analysis A study of whether a form is needed and what static information it should contain, in what sequence and design.

Forms file A file used for the storage of either blank or filled-out forms.

Freedom of Information Act A law that allows people to see information kept on file about themselves.

Frequency of reference How often a file might be used.

Geographic filing An alphabetic arrangement of records by location.

Given name An individual's first name.

Guide A sheet of heavy cardboard with a tab and caption, used to guide the eye to the desired section in a file drawer. A guide also serves as a support for the records in the drawer.

Guide rod A metal rod included in most file drawers that is placed through the guide rod extension in the bottom of the guides to hold them in place within the file drawer.

Guide rod extension A projection at the bottom center of a guide that contains a metal-reinforced hole in the middle through which a guide rod is placed within the file drawer.

Guide words See *Static information.*

HFA file Another name for a tickler or follow-up file. The initials stand for "Hold for action" or "Hold for answer."

Hanging folders See *Suspended folders*.

Hard copy Material which is in paper and print form instead of in film or magnetic media.

"Hold for answer" file See *HFA file*.

Hyphenated name An individual or firm name that consists of words or letters connected by a hyphen. Both a hyphenated surname and a hyphenated firm name are considered as one unit for indexing.

"In," "Out," and "Hold" Baskets See *Desk trays*.

Inactive records Records not subject to frequent use that are stored in less accessible and less costly equipment than active records.

Index card record A card, such as an address file card, that is used primarily as a reference to other information.

Indexing Selecting the caption under which a record is to be filed.

Indexing arrangement The order in which the units of a name are considered for filing.

Indirect A filing system that usually requires reference to an index before records can be found.

Individual folder A folder that contains records concerning only one correspondent or subject.

Information maintenance Keeping data in a form that makes it usable.

Information processing Changing the form of data to make it usable.

Information retrieval Getting information out of a manual or electronic storage device.

Input The information put into a business system.

Inspecting Checking the correspondence for a release mark before storing.

Kraft Heavyweight paper used for file guides and folders.

Label A sticker that is attached to the tab of a guide or a folder and on which the caption appears.

Lamination Permanently enclosing a record in clear plastic.

Landscaped office See *Open office*.

Lateral file A file cabinet in which records are stored perpendicular to the opening of the file.

Letterhead Stationery with a printed heading.

Logbook A notebook containing records of important business transactions. A logbook may be used to record incoming and outgoing mail, telephone calls, or other business transactions.

Main numeric file The primary file in a system using numbers. This file contains individual folders that are placed behind the appropriate guide. Inside these folders, records are maintained in chronological order with the most recent record in front.

Manila Medium-weight pressboard used for file folders.

Maximum-minimum transfer A plan for periodically transferring records from active to transfer files. A maximum and a minimum period of time are set for storing records in active files.

Merging Combining the contents of two or more folders into one, either using the caption of one of the old folders or creating a new caption to cover the new combination of contents.

Method A breakdown of a procedure into the steps by which it is accomplished. See *System*.

Microfacsimile Transmission of data on microfiche or aperture cards over telephone lines to produce hard copy at the other end.

Microfiche Miniature filmed records in card form.

Microfilm A roll of microimages.

Microfilming The photographing of records at greatly reduced size on film-strips, cards, or rolls. The film can be maintained in only 2 percent of the space required for the original records.

Microform Either film or paper which contains microimages.

Micrographics Reproduction of information on microforms.

Microimage Reduction of a larger record or document.

Micropublishing Production of information on microforms for public use, either for sale or for free distribution.

Microrepublishing Reproducing of information previously in hard-copy form for public use.

Middle-digit filing A numeric arrangement of records according to the middle, rather than the first, digits.

Miscellaneous alphabetic file The part of a numeric file used for those correspondents for whom sufficient records have not accumulated to merit a number being assigned to them.

Miscellaneous folder A folder that contains records for correspondents or subjects not active enough to warrant individual folders.

Misfile To store a record in the wrong location.

Multiple transfer See *Two-period transfer.*

Name file A card file containing identifying information about names.

Need to know The term used to refer to the job duties of those persons allowed access to confidential records.

Numeric correspondence file A filing system organized in three parts: a main numeric file, a miscellaneous alphabetic file, and a card index in which the names of correspondents or subjects are arranged alphabetically.

Numeric filing The filing of correspondence or cards according to numbers.

Numeric subject file A basic kind of subject file that includes several systems that use numbers for captions in place of words.

One-period transfer A plan in which the active files contain records for the current filing period only. At predetermined intervals all the records are transferred.

Open office The landscaped office arrangement in which several employees occupy a large room divided by furniture or partitions to form work groups or to allow various configurations of equipment.

Open-shelf filing A method of filing in which shelves, rather than filing cabinets with drawers, are used to house records.

Out folder A folder used to store correspondence while the regular folder is out of the files. It indicates that the regular folder has been borrowed and gives the name of the borrower.

Out guide A guide used to indicate that an entire folder has been removed from the files.

Paperless office An organization that changes correspondence and business records in electronic or micrographic media to carry on everyday business activities.

Pending file A file containing matters which are not yet completed and upon which some action must be taken.

Periodic transfer The removal of records at predetermined intervals from the current active files to the inactive or transfer files.

Perpetual transfer The transfer of records from current to inactive files on the basis of activity rather than predetermined filing periods.

Political division An area created by law, such as a town, city, county, state, or nation.

Position The location, counting from left to right, of the tab on a guide or folder.

Possessive A word indicating ownership; usually contains an apostrophe. In indexing, the letter *s* after the apostrophe is considered.

Posted card records Card files that are used to record new information on a continuous basis.

Power file units Files which bring the desired shelf to the user automatically.

Prefix A word element, such as *Mc,* at the beginning of a word or name.

Preposition A word used to connect a noun or a pronoun with some other word. Prepositions, such as *for, in,* and *of,* are disregarded in indexing.

Primary guide The main guide for a section of filed records.

Priorities Those items of work which are more important than others. Setting priorities means ranking the order of importance of the jobs or tasks which must be done and doing the most important first.

Privacy Act A law that allows individuals to designate which people may see records and information kept on file about themselves.

Procedure A series of related substeps performed to carry out part of a system. See *System.*

Procedures manual Description of the filing system and pertinent information for all users.

Protection Storing records in equipment for safekeeping in the event of a fire or other disaster.

Punched card A 7⅜ by 3¼-inch card record that is coded with small punched holes and processed on data processing machines.

Reader A machine used to view microfilms or microfiche.

Reading file Extra copies of outgoing correspondence.

Recharge form A slip used to charge out records when they are passed from one person to another without being returned to the files.

Records All information that is kept by an organization, whether it is in the form of correspondence, cards, tapes, or microforms.

Records control Procedures used to keep track of records after they have been created or received and stored in the files.

Records inventory A statement of the kinds of material and folders in the files, the quantity of those records, and their location.

Records management Planning, organizing, and controlling the creation, protection, use, storage, and disposition of records.

Records manager An individual who oversees the operation of the records system, including the active files and the charge system, and who establishes the transfer and retention procedures and has the authority to destroy obsolete records.

Reference The directing of an individual's attention to a source of information.

Register A list of correspondents and the numbers assigned to them in a numeric correspondence file.

Relative index An alphabetic list of all the headings and subheadings in a subject file.

Release mark A notation showing that a record has received the required attention and is ready for filing.

Requisition slip A form used to request records from the files.

Retention period A period of time during which records are kept in either active or transfer files before they are destroyed.

Retrieval Finding—the major goal of any filing system.

Rotary files Round shelves attached to a center pole, which can be turned for easy access; also small desktop files on a wheel.

Routing form A slip attached to charged-out records indicating the sequence in which they are to be delivered to several individuals in an organization before being returned to the files.

Safes Vertical correspondence files with combination locks, made of fireproof and protective materials.

Scores Creases along the front flap of a folder that allow for expansion.

Secondary guide A guide that subdivides the section of a file controlled by a primary guide.

Security center An underground or isolated storage place for very valuable records.

Selective copying A feature of multiple-copy specialty forms that prevents some of the information recorded on the first sheet from being copied on other sheets.

Self-mailer A form designed so that it can be mailed back to the sender without being placed in an envelope.

Sequence A logical order, either according to the letters of the alphabet or according to numbers.

Signals Plastic, metal, or paper devices that are used to guide the eye to pertinent information, usually in card and visible files.

Simple numeric A type of numeric filing system that uses only nine divisions or subdivisions under the same heading.

Single caption A caption that indicates only where the section of the file starts. Only one letter or one combination of letters appears.

Sorting Arranging records in sequence after they have been coded to facilitate storing.

Soundex A commercial numeric filing system that brings together in the files all names that sound alike but may be spelled differently.

Special guide See *Secondary guide*.

Staggered arrangement Placement of guide or folder tabs in successive positions from left to right.

Static information All the printed information on a form before it is filled in.

Storing The placing of records in a file container.

Subject filing The alphabetic arrangement of records by names of topics or things.

Substitution card A card used to replace records removed from a file folder. This card indicates the name of the borrower.

Summary A record of the business transactions that take place while an employer is away from the office.

Supervisor The person who is responsible for the operation and maintenance of files and filing systems.

Surname The last name of an individual.

Surname prefix That part of a surname that precedes the body of the surname, such as *De, Fitz, Mac, O'*, and *Von*. These prefixes are indexed as part of the surname.

Suspended folders Folders supported from their top edges by a metal frame within the file drawer.

Suspense file A follow-up or tickler file used for items which need action in the future.

System A series of related steps followed in accomplishing a major office activity. A procedure is a series of related substeps performed to carry out part of a system. For example, the procedure for figuring hours worked from a timecard is part of the larger payroll system.

Tab The projection above the body of a guide or folder on which the caption appears.

Template A scale-size cutout or stencil of equipment; used in planning layouts.

Terminal-digit filing A numeric arrangement of records according to the last, rather than the first, digits.

Tickler file A follow-up file, usually organized by date.

Time stamp See *Date stamp*.

Title A word indicating rank, office, or privilege. A title is considered an indexing unit only when it precedes a single name or is part of a firm name.

"To Do" list List of items which need attention within the next day or so.

Topical filing See *Subject filing*.

Traditional office The enclosed office space occupied by one or more individuals.

Transfer Removal of records from the active files to inactive files.

Transfer file or box A container that houses transferred records. This container is usually constructed of inexpensive cardboard or metal materials.

Transpose To rearrange the normal order of a name; for example, *Donald Windham* transposed is *Windham, Donald*.

Triple-digit A numeric arrangement of records according to the last three digits.

Tub files Containers which open at the top to expose records suspended in folders or in trays.

Two-period transfer A plan in which the active files provide space for current records and records from the last filing period. At transfer time, only the oldest records are removed.

Unit Each part of a name used in indexing.

Unit record A single identifiable piece of information, often a punched card.

Variable information Data filled in on a form. Also known as *fill-ins* or *fill-in information*.

Variadex A commercial color filing system.

Vertical filing The storage of records on edge.

Visible filing Storage of cards in specially designed equipment so that the information near the edges of the cards can be seen easily.

Word processing A means of processing written information within an organization by using special automated typewriters for fast, efficient production.

Word processing log A logbook kept in the word processing department in which a record is made of all incoming work. Logs are also kept for information that is recorded on magnetic media for various machines.

Work station The location of one employee's equipment and materials (desk, chair, file, etc.) in an office.

Work-in-progress file Contains one or more projects which have not yet been completed and which may require periodic attention.

Index